D1076312

It's all about pussy...

Welcome to *Pussy*, the magazine for cats that should know better. This month, we explore serious issues that affect us all, like Millie, that minx who won the Cat Show… phwoar! And as if that's not enough to get you rubbing against furniture purring like a Geiger counter in a nuclear power plant, then check out Dixie. Exotic or wot?

Elsewhere, we trace the history and cultural significance of that perennial garden favourite, catnip. For your interest, it took approximately 17 ounces of pure grade catnip to put this issue of *Pussy* together. Tibbles, the art editor, is drooling in the stationery cupboard on the look-out for imaginary mice as I type this. Poor deluded fool.

For those of you who think you're hard, we journey into the badlands of Big Farm to investigate the feral phenomenon. We also take another look at the terrible murders committed by history's most notorious serial killer, Spike The Dog, with an exclusive interview with Tiddles, the investigating officer of the Babes In The Tube murders. It's not for the faint-hearted, but we here at *Pussy* take our commitment to hard-hitting journalism seriously.

But don't worry if that's too heavy for you, as the rest of the mag is largely devoted to pussy cat essentials like 33 Things You Never Knew About Goldfish, Great Bins Of Our Time, the *Pussy* guide to human persons, and a bunch of other nonsense we made up at the last minute.

Pussy, you love it.

Me, yesterday

PAWS

Editor Perry
Deputy editor Arthur Big Bollox
Art editor Tibbles
Production editor Fuzz
Chief sub editor Catface Killa
Staff writer Nobby
Designer Pebbles
Picture editor Frank The Cat
Picture assistant Ginger
Tea cats Dave and his cousin Fluffy

Advertising manager Smiffy
Advertising executive Amber
Classified sales Burper
Group advertising director Monghead

Contributors Millie, Perry, Minski, Taisha, Kishi, Puss de Wuss, Tabitha, Tiddles, Dixie, Purdy, Spike, Paul Daniels, Terminator, Casper, Phoebe, Maru-chan, Mork, Mindy, Bob, Ludo, Tizzy, Minty, Pugsley, Minnie, Flo, Dotty, Samba, Daphne Mae, Basil, Sidney, Coco, Thomas, Chip, Dale, Brandy, Bianca, Koshka, Inca, Fatty, Didz, Cooper
Dogs Emmie, Indigo, Alfie
Ferrets (Long Rabbits) Gunner, Jager, Jasmine, Bear
All Hamsters Hammy

Contact us at:
The Garden Shed
The House With The Red Door
Big Town
M1 A0W

This month's contributors

MOGGINS
Moggins is features editor of *Furtive* magazine and is probably the best known crime reporter in the country. He is six.

RATTER
The award-winning travel writer looks for fun beyond the hedge on page 100. He also writes for *I Will Eat You* and *The Daily Wiz.*

GERALD
Goldfish expert Gerald has spent his entire life studying aquatic life of all kinds. He has eaten 74 goldfish and one koi carp.

CONTENTS

90

84

REGULARS

8 **Letters**

10 **Scratching Post**
Bags of fun from all over Big Town

42 **Competition**

44 **Perverts**
A tale of depraved love so shocking you'll chunder

96 **Sport**
A ringside report from the Big Fight and an exploration of football violence

100 **Travel**
With our award-winning correspondent Ratter

106 **Fashion**

116 **Grooming**

120 **Problems**

122 **Horoscopes**
What has Spooky Sparkles got in store for you this month?

124 **Readers' Mates**

FEATURES

46 **Millie**
Big Town's hottest starlet reveals all for *Pussy*

54 **Catnip**
Our hard-hitting investigation discovers that it's good for you

62 **Sleep**
Another hard-hitting investigation discovers that this is good for you, too

68 **Spooky Twins**
Sinister duo Saturn and Mercury confuse us all

76 **Feral Kulture**
A close encounter with the violent gang from the Big Farm

84 **Killer Dog**
The story of infamous serial killer Spike. He was probably innocent, but we're not too bothered

90 **Dixie**
Southern fried fun with this lady from across the pond

10

96

46

76

68

120

106

The Vulvo V990

The ride of our lives

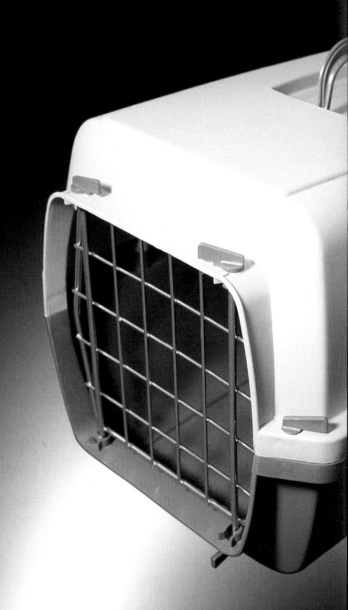

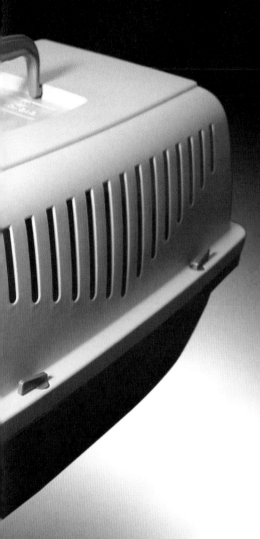

Air conditioned. Easy-wipe plastic. Smooth handling.
You wouldn't even mind going to the vets in this beauty

A computer hacker, a stinky wazzer and an old duffer all contribute to this issue. To have your say, write to: *Pussy* Letters, The Garden Shed, The House With The Red Door, Big Town M1 A0W

STAR LETTER

Dear *Pussy*,
While my person went off and left me on my own for a weekend, I sneaked onto his stupid computer and drew this picture of me doing a shit. I then hacked into the root code for the system (which, for the technically minded among your readers, is located in the boot ROM on the C-drive) and made the picture the computer's permanent desktop image. He can't delete it, and he's got a big Powerpoint presentation on Tuesday to his bosses, so they'll see my drawing of me doing a shit and probably sack him. That'll teach him for leaving me on my own with nothing but a bowl of dried food to get me through, the bastard.
Pieface, Big Town
Ed sez: Here's Pieface's charming self-portrait. Have any other readers managed to make some art they would like to send us? If the art is offensive, or has caused considerable embarrassment, or has had serious financial implications for a person, then so much the better.

STINKY WAZ
Dear *Pussy*,
Yesterday, I did a really stinky waz all over the corner of the sofa in the living room.
Ginge, Big Town
Ed sez: Well done, Ginge. But remember, don't make a habit of it, otherwise you might find yourself getting put down for having 'kidney trouble'. We have a reputation to maintain as clean domestic pets, and while it might not always be convenient, it's the best way to guarantee a lifetime of free food and warm places to sleep.

THE OLD DAYS
Sirs,
It has recently come to my attention that your publication and others like it are propagating lifestyle choices which are threatening to undermine a way of life that was once common in Big Town. I can remember when cats had time for one another, and it wasn't all "fucking this" and "fucking that", and when you get up in the morning, "oh, fuck this". In my day, cats would respect one another's territories and we'd follow the person police at night when they patrolled the beat. Very occasionally we would knock a dustbin lid to the ground and yowl, but that was simply for a bit of local colour. The sort of individualism that seems to inform the 'me' culture of young cats today has its roots in the kind of stories that are printed in *Pussy*. It really is quite disturbing. I urge you to consider the influence you have, and to concentrate rather less on the vulgar urges of the unsophisticated cat, and more on notions of decorum and mutual respect.
Yours faithfully,
Dodds, Big Town
Ed sez: Shove it up your arse, grandad!

LEAVE US ALONE

Oi *Pussy*!

I'm the hardest cat in Big Town and I'm well mental, too. There's nothing I wouldn't do. I'll eat anything and I can lay a coil on demand anywhere you like. I'm also a very prolific fur ball spewer. Can I have a job on your magazine?

Jack, Big Town

Ed sez: No.

SINISTER EVIL COLONY

Sirs,

In my attempts to build a colony based on domination using violence, I have found it necessary to consume three alpha males, making a grandiose display of eating their brains from their tiny skulls. The tactic worked and now I am the unquestioned overlord of my world. However, I was wondering whether you might have any advice on disposing of body remains which are inedible. I'm thinking specifically about partly gnawed bones and pelts which are encrusted with the dried blood of my victims. Also, the lengthy article about the removal of political opposition in the last issue of *The Wheel* recommended the introduction of martial law before the abolition of freedom of assembly, whereas I find the reverse strategy can hasten victory by several days.

Hammy The Hamster, Big Town

Ed sez: Every now and then we receive mail which was intended for another publication. Clearly Hammy here was hoping his letter would be read and answered by those little bastards at The Wheel *magazine. Frankly, they have always given us the creeps, and now we know why.*

MAD GINGER FUCKER

Dear *Pussy*,

They've put trellis up on the fence at Number 54 and it has totally ruined my fucking life. Now when I'm senselessly pacing around my territory three or four times a day, I have to go around the front of the houses past that mad ginger fucker who waits on the window sill and attacks anything that goes within 10 feet of him. Honestly, people are complete wankers, aren't they?

Greg, Big Town

Ed sez: Except at meal times.

HAIRY IDIOT

Puss de Wuss, yesterday

Dear *Pussy*,

I think I look like Puss de Wuss from Number 36. What do your readers think?

Puss de Wuss, Big Town

Ed sez: You are Puss de Wuss from Number 36, you blithering idiot.

DOG END

Pussykins!

I've discovered that if I stand upright on my back legs and miaow a few times and possibly even throw in a bit of purring, the people here will often give me food, like fish or cheese. Especially if I follow them from room to room. Once, I got some spaghetti – which was all right, actually. It tasted a bit like chicken, only without the chickeny flavour.

Herman, Big Town

Ed sez: Whoah, there! Standing on your hind legs? Begging for food? Why not howl at the moon and go for walkies with a noose around your neck, too? What's the matter with you? Have some dignity, for flip's sake.

WHO SMELLS?

Dear *Pussy*,

You smell.

Anon, Big Town

Ed sez: No, you smell.

COLD FEET

Dear *Pussy*,

Me and my mates all went out on the razz the other night. We knocked dustbin lids over, fought with the mangy cats from the derelict house, had a fur ball hurling up competition and generally went apeshit. The problem is, when we got home, we'd lost our mittens. Has anyone seen them?

The Kittens, Big Town

Ed sez: Can you help? Let us know at the usual address.

BOHEMIAN RHAPSODY

Hello *Pussy*,

I just went to London to see the Queen and all she did was shout "Get ite, get ite, you horrid little creature," and set her corgis on me, the silly old moo.

Pussy Cat Pussy Cat, Big Town

Ed sez: Are you taking the piss, or what?

POINTLESS SPACE FILLER

Dear *Pussy*,

Re your article about eating birds (*Eating Birds – Isn't It All Just A Bit Too Feathery?*). Your inability to recognise the difference between a chicken and a turkey is quite understandable, but there are some tell-tail signs. A chicken is quite small and goes "cluck-cluck-cluck". A turkey, by contrast, is fucking enormous and goes "gobble-gobble-gobble".

Sir Eat-A-Lot, Big Town

Ed sez: Thanks for clearing that up.

WHAT UP!

Dear *Pussy*,

I wrote this letter in mouse blood. Do I win anything?

Hannibal, Big Town Penitentiary

Ed sez: We are sending you something wet which you might enjoy with a nice Chianti. Fafafafafa.

SCRATCHING
POST

SPIGGY CLIMBS STICK SHOCKER!

There was jubilation yesterday when Spiggy climbed all the way to the top of the big scratching post in the try-outs for the Big Town Olympic team.

"I've been in training for a year now," he told the waiting press scrum after he'd come down backwards, looking considerably less confident than he had on the way up. When he got to the top, he sort of hung there with his ears flat against his head, looking around like a nutter. "I was confident I could make it this time," said Spiggy. "I've been climbing up the back of the sofa regularly and have got pretty good at it."

Spiggy's climbing talents represent the best chance for Big Town to scoop a medal in the forthcoming Olympics, after the relay team collapsed in disarray. Fat Face bit Sooty on the tail, so Sooty went home all pissed off.

THINGS TO KILL
No. 17: Frogs

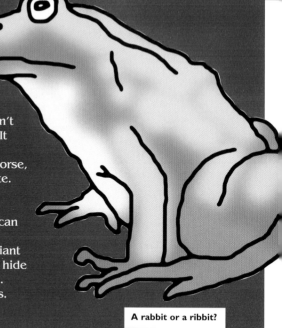

What is a frog? A green ball on legs.
Do what? Run that by me again? A frog's got legs but it doesn't know how to use them properly. Run is the last thing it can do. It bounces around like a ball instead.
Sounds weird. Is it easy to catch? Nope. To make matters worse, it often lives near water. And, as we all know, water is nasty shite.
Eugh! Is it worth the risk? Does it taste good?
Not especially. It tastes like chicken.
So why bother with it? It's alive, isn't it? Which means that it can be made dead.
Fair enough. What else? The best thing is that it makes a brilliant squealing noise when you squeeze it. If you catch one at night, hide in a cupboard with it and squeeze away. It'll terrify your person.
Not to be confused with: French cats, balls, chickens, rabbits.

Next issue: WORMS

A rabbit or a ribbit?

THE PUSSY FOOD CHALLENGE

Our resident gourmand T[...] the lot, and puts on anoth[...]

	PRESENTATION	BEST ENJOYED...
TINNED FOOD	Emits person-nauseating odour when opened, particularly rabbit flavour. Tastes a bit like chicken, except for the chicken flavour, which tastes like tuna.	From the floor next to the bowl it was served in. This is considered good etiquette and your person will enjoy cleaning the kitchen floor as you walk off with your tail in the air for a nice dump in the flower bed.
ORGANIC FOOD	Ah, the thrill of the chase! Those satisfying spurts of blood! Ears not recommended. Worms don't seem to have ears, though. Not even tiny ones. They don't have eyes, either. Or feet. Easier to catch than mice, because they can't hear you. Or run away. Note that birds can fly. Bastards.	In the garden, in the alley, anywhere you like. Eating *al fresco* is always a delight, but tearing a small defenceless creature limb from limb in front of your person adds a certain piquancy to the dining experience which they will admire you for.
PERSON FOOD	Sossiges are nice. Cheese is nice. Oranges are nasty and pasta is pointless.	Handed to you by a doting person as you pester them and go miaow a lot. They love that.

CATWOMAN
WHO ARE THEY KIDDING?

Catwoman? I ask you. There's an immediate problem with the name. Cat? Fine. Woman? Not good. The two don't go together, do they? But that's not the only outrageous faux paws. Latex? Really? Since when did cats have latex skin? And Catwoman's arch-enemy is Batman, is it? If it was Dogman, maybe they'd have a point. A big stupid dog running around the place wearing a cape and a utility belt would put the willies up me. But a bat?! Do me a favour. My mate Carlos ate 16 bats one day. For breakfast. They taste a bit like chicken, apparently. And Robin?! Pah!! Since when were robins yellow and green? Robins appear at Christmas and have red breasts. Any idiot knows that. They taste a bit like chicken. And these Hollywood buffoons would have us believe there's a bird called a Penguin. There are no such things as penguins. Have you ever met one? Hold on a second... Oh... It seems that penguins do exist. They live on ice and taste a bit like chicken. Fair enough. Still, Catwoman, eh? Who are they kidding?

Next issue: CATWEAZLE

1000 REASONS WHY DOGS ARE STUPID
PART 82

757. Barking. Woof! Woof! Woof! Oh yes, very articulate, Mr Wilde.
758. Slobber. Yeuch.
759. "Fetch! Fetch the stick!"
760. Hmm, look Mr Dog, a lovely lump of another dog's faeces – yum yum!
761. Leads – without which a dog will run straight into the path of the nearest speeding bus. There's a good reason why they call you Bozo, Bozo.
762. The moon. Here's an idea: why don't you howl at it?
763. Body odour.
764. Man's best friend? Dumb and dumber, more like.

...t eats more food. This time, he tackles tinned, organic and person grub, scoffs ...x pounds. Way to go, Tubcat!

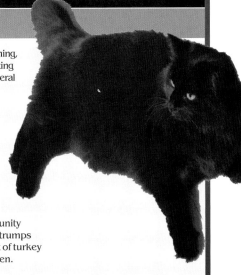

SICK FACTOR

Tinned food can produce copious amounts of sticky spew which, when combined with the vomit/reverse technique more usually employed for hacking up fur balls, will result in a nice long trail of sick.

More likely to produce vomit in your person, which is always worth the effort.

Be careful when vomiting up person food. They might assume it means you don't like it. It doesn't mean you don't like it. You're just being sick, that's all.

THE VERDICT

A good all-rounder for day-to-day munching, but do remember to combine with hunting and occasionally leave a bowlful for several days without touching it. Ultimately, tinned food tastes better from the neighbour's cat bowl than your own.

Let's face it, this is the best. The downside is availability and the fact that you have to get up off your arse and chase stuff around like a twat before stuffing your face.

Rarely anything more than an opportunity to annoy your person, but comes up trumps around Christmas, when there's a lot of turkey around. Turkey tastes a bit like chicken.

HOME ENTERTAINMENT

Fun for you, hell for them!

Frank (from The House With The White Door)
"My person had been writing for about a year and was mumbling about his 'novel', so I found the file on the hard drive, selected all the text (90,000 words!) and replaced it with my own creative writing. Boy, was he ever pissed off! Result!"

Tiswas (from Number 106)
"I just love to wait for my person to put his anorak on and leave the door to his hobby room open. I walk around all the very finely detailed plastic things that he has spent so much time building (he even avoids getting glue on the clear bits) and knock into them. Sometimes I even have a quick chew. He always goes red when he gets back with yet another box of plastic. Result!"

EIGHT SPECTACULAR

Life is full of hazards, pussy cats, so take care. Cut out and keep *Pussy*

Jumping from tower blocks

Napping under cars

Chewing electric cables

Crossing the road

Thomas (from Number 16)

"My people came back from a holiday somewhere and insisted on parading their shockingly bad taste by placing a cat ornament they'd picked up at some tawdry market on the mantelpiece. They were very proud of it and thought it was the best thing they'd ever bought. Then, one night, I crept up onto the mantelpiece and knocked the hideous piece of crap onto the floor, where it smashed into lots of little sharp bits. My people came running down the stairs thinking there was an intruder and they both cut their feet on their rubbish ornament. Hahaha. Result!"

Rankin (from Number 90)

"All I meant to do was knock a few glasses over when my over-protective and neurotic person had set the table for a dinner party. But because I'd been stomping about in the litter tray, I wiped traces of my faecal matter all over the cutlery – with the result that all the guests contracted a virulent stomach bug. My person now has no friends. Not one. Result!"

WAYS TO LOSE A LIFE

ry own guide to things you might want to avoid when out and about

Lapping bleach

Getting sick and dying

Dog aggro

Napping in a washing machine

LIONS AND TIGERS: FACT OR FICTION?

CONFUSED AND DELUDED

YOSSER: "Lions and tigers? Load of cobblers, if you ask me. And I should know. I'm a really adventurous cat – I've been to the end of the street and everything – and I've never come across one."

SAM: "I don't know about tigers, but I've definitely seen a lion. At the vets. It had sharp teeth and evil eyes. It was terrifying. It talked about killing all the time. And there was something disturbing about the way that it ran round its little wheel thing. I think it was called Hammy. Yeah, Hammy The Lion..."

LOUIS: "I used to have a tiger living in my house. It died years ago. Before I was born. It ate too much tuna one night and exploded in front of the fire. KA-BOOM! It's still there now. I like to sleep on it. And I've got a hippopottomouse living next door. It keeps putting its head through the wall."

SIMBA SAYS: "I REALLY IS A TIGER"

It's a jungle out there. Does it make you wonder sometimes, how you keep from going under?
"Uh-huh-huh, uh-huh-huh. It was even more of a jungle when I first moved in here, but my person got busy with the rake. Not that I approve. I like it wild."
What's the wildest you've ever been?
"Oh, I'm wild all the time. You have no idea. I've lost count of the number of shrubs I've destroyed."
Have you always had an exploring spirit?
"Yeah. One garden's never been enough for me. Even as a kitten, I'd roam three or four gardens – in every direction. As far as I'm concerned, fences are just for jumping over. Well, that and sitting on."
You're a fast runner, aren't you?
"Like the clappers. It's because I really is a tiger."
But you haven't got stripes. You've got spots.
"Is it measles?"
No, not those kind of spots. You're spotty like a leopard. Like a leopard is spotty. You shouldn't even be here. This is about lions and tigers, not leopards. We'll have to ask you to leave now...

VOTE NOW

FIREMAN OF THE YEAR AWARD

Hold on to your branches, kitties! Yes, it's time to get your votes in for *Pussy*'s prestigious Fireman Of The Year Award. Which of Big Town's Firemen has the longest ladder? We have three candidates vying for your support. They are:
a) The tall one
b) The other tall one
c) The short one with warm hands
Send your votes to our usual address. The award will be presented by Sherpa, up the tree behind Number 57, next Wednesday.

bogwater

brewed in Bigtown since last Friday

Where there's a flush there's a rush

dead mice

We're Eatin' 'em

Big Mouse – The original
Small Shrew – For those who like a small portion with a bit of tanginess
Hammyburger – Non free-range fully fat hammies. Tastes like chicken
Double Gerbil – Tastes like two chickens

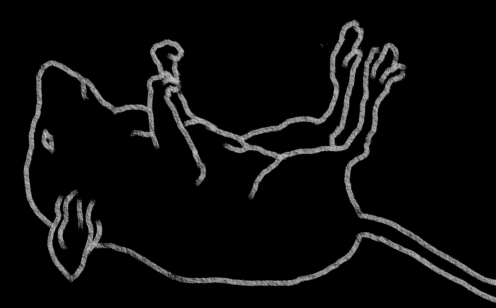

All our products contain 100% pure rodent and will also include the horrible browny-purple bit that you might like to leave behind

bob's bit

Bob the Urban Kitten goes for a tumble

Yo homeys![1] Fo' shizzle my kizzle![2] This month, I have mostly been brocking out[3] to some abstract beats laid down by the washing machine massive[4] in the kitchen. Tune![5] I met Perkins and I told him I woz going for the washing machine spin. And he called me a twat, so I brocked[6] him. Ba-zing![7] So anyway, I woz feeling the abstract shizzle[8] of the washing machine when a thought occurred to me: what would happen if I ran around in circles for three minutes? So I did. And it makes you go blazza[9] and fall over. Then I went on a hench[10] merk[11] spree, and killed a worm. And it wasn't even time for din-dins yet. So then I went to sleep and I dreamed about the burned-out car I used to live in. Then I woke up and I went total yabbadabbadoo[12] and ran around in circles for ages and ages. Blimey! Talk about exciting. Woop! Woop! The sound of da po-lice![13] So which is best, the washing machine massive or running around in circles? The washing machine, you pingo![14] Duh! That made me spew! See you next month!

BOB'S GLOSSARY

1: Hello readers!
2: How pleasant to greet you, my kitten friend
3: Very much enjoying making mad faces while dancing
4: The washing machine
5: I enjoyed that music
6: Made a mad, scary face
7: Onomatopoeia; the sound made when one brocks another
8: Sounds
9: Onomatopoeia; the sound of vomiting. From "blargh!"
10: Large/huge, appalling, monstrous, bang out of order
11: Murder
12: Mental
13: Lyrics from popular rap star KRS-One's *Sound Of Da Police*
14: A foolish fellow

PEOPLE

DOES YOUR PERSON...

- Feed you red salmon in vinegar?
- Have her TV deafeningly loud?
- Have a croaky voice and knobbly feet?
- Smell of cabbage?
- Sleep all evening?
- Take you on the bus in a cardboard box?

YOUR PERSON IS AN OLD LADY

Life with this person: That tartan material she puts on her lap is a bit rough and the lino on the kitchen floor is a bastard on the pads in the winter. There are definite advantages to owning an old lady, though. She is always available for cuddles and it only takes one miaow for the tin opener to magically appear in her hand. She lights a nice real fire when it gets really cold, too.

🐾 🐾 🐾 🐾 🐾 🐾 🐾 🐾

DOES YOUR PERSON...

- Come in a pair?
- Disappear for days on end?
- Call you 'darling'?
- Cuddle you when they're drunk?
- Feed you dry food pellets and bits of poncey vol-au-venty things?

YOUR PERSONS ARE A TRENDY CHILDLESS COUPLE

Life with these persons: Infuriating. Where do they keep disappearing to? Why are they a different colour when they come back? And why won't they let you go in the nice big garden? Still, at least it's easy to wrap them round your little claw. Especially the male. Rolling around in a cutesy way never fails to impress the soppy dolt. And don't forget to indulge in lots of noisy arse licking when they're having dinner.

🐾 🐾 🐾 🐾 🐾 🐾

20 **PUSSY**

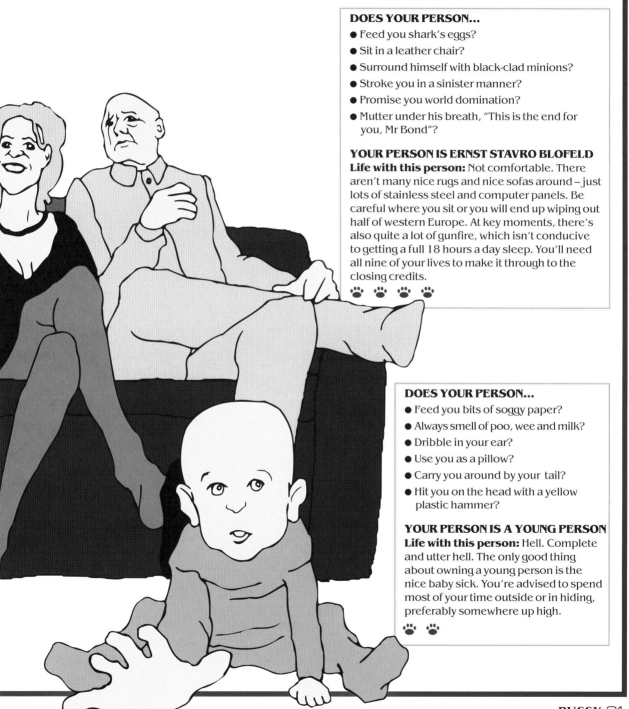

DOES YOUR PERSON...

- Feed you shark's eggs?
- Sit in a leather chair?
- Surround himself with black-clad minions?
- Stroke you in a sinister manner?
- Promise you world domination?
- Mutter under his breath, "This is the end for you, Mr Bond"?

YOUR PERSON IS ERNST STAVRO BLOFELD
Life with this person: Not comfortable. There aren't many nice rugs and nice sofas around – just lots of stainless steel and computer panels. Be careful where you sit or you will end up wiping out half of western Europe. At key moments, there's also quite a lot of gunfire, which isn't conducive to getting a full 18 hours a day sleep. You'll need all nine of your lives to make it through to the closing credits.

DOES YOUR PERSON...

- Feed you bits of soggy paper?
- Always smell of poo, wee and milk?
- Dribble in your ear?
- Use you as a pillow?
- Carry you around by your tail?
- Hit you on the head with a yellow plastic hammer?

YOUR PERSON IS A YOUNG PERSON
Life with this person: Hell. Complete and utter hell. The only good thing about owning a young person is the nice baby sick. You're advised to spend most of your time outside or in hiding, preferably somewhere up high.

CAT DISCOVERS NEW DIMENSION

Poppy from Number 95 has reported seeing a gateway to a new dimension where her metaphysical form divided into many facets. "My metaphyscial form divided into many facets," she told an astonished gathering of interested parties at the annual Science Fair Expo. However, Professor Bartlett, author of the acclaimed *When The Wind Blows, I Go Mad*, accused Poppy of being a charlatan. "She's a charlatan," he said. "The evidence she presented to support her frankly outrageous claims was patchy at best. She's a laughing stock. I hate her."

Controversy has dogged the Science Fair Expo since its inauguration last year, when Poppy presented a thesis on cats originating in space, and Professor Bartlett sat at the back and laughed all the way through. They then faced each other up on the fence at Number 87 and swished their tails for 10 minutes, but there was no fight.

Poppy's metaphysical facets

3 things to do before you're 3

1) Climb to the top of the curtains. Hang off, lean back and look really crazy.

2) Kill a big gnat (the ones that you usually find dead anyway). Dismember it and eat its abdomen only.

3) Attempt a leap from the first-floor window to the other first-floor window.

BOX OF KITTENS
The winner of our Box of Kittens contest is Minty (and his mates)

The Fireside Storyteller
Tales from The Fireplace

The little kittens settled down in expectation of their nightly fairy tale. But once again, The Fireside Storyteller was fast asleep by the end of the second sentence.

Zzzzz...

Comfort...

33 THINGS YOU NEVER KNEW ABOUT

GOLDFISHO

✂ They are made out of fish, but they are not made out of gold

✂ Some are more orange than gold. Which is actually yellow, anyway

✂ But orangefish doesn't sound right

✂ Neither does yellowfish

✂ Goldfish look a bit like carrots

✂ They breathe water through their mouths and expel it out of their arses, which propels them along

✂ Goldfish, that is, not carrots

✂ Bubbles, the goldfish at Number 63, called Tom a "wanker". Which is why Tom ate him

✂ Come to think of it, what are those black fish called you see in goldfish bowls?

✂ Oh, apparently they're goldfish, too

✂ The black fish also taste of fish (thanks to Marbles from The House With The Curtains Always Closed for the info on black fish)

✂ The best way to eat goldfish is to sit over the bowl and stare for a while as they swim about

✂ Then sort of half put your paw in the bowl, let it dangle there before it gets wet, then pretend like you're not going to actually bother trying to hook one of the little bastards

✂ Then suddenly stick your paw in the water and flip a goldfish out

✂ As it thrashes about on the floor (and before your person comes storming in and makes everything very confusing with all the shouting and stuff), grab it in your mouth and run away

✂ Eat the fish

✂ This also works with goldfish that live in ponds

✂ Those really big fish you sometimes see in ponds aren't goldfish

✂ They might be tuna

✂ But we're not sure

✂ Or maybe cod

✂ Apparently, there's a fish called a catfish

✂ And another one called a dogfish, which is really stupid. Arf! Arf!

✂ Have you ever considered the irony of the fact that our favourite food in the world is fish and yet, as a species, we are burdened with a genetic hatred of water – which makes catching them a deeply unpleasant experience?

✂ Tchoh! It's so unfair. How come I have to come up with 33 things about goldfish? Is it because you didn't like my hororscopes page?

✂ The Latin name for goldfish, which is what doctors call them, is *goldusfishus*

✂ Goldfish live in underwater castles called Blobbies. Oh yes they do

✂ When a goldfish dies, the other goldfish put the dead body on a longboat, set it on fire and push it out onto The Big Pond. For this ceremony, they all wear traditional Viking helmets

✂ At other times when a goldfish dies, your person flushes them down the toilet, which seems to be a terrible waste

✂ Modern goldfish bowls have small goldfish-shaped flaps hidden round the back so they can go out and do their toilet and meet other goldfish

✂ Is that 33 yet? I want to go out to play

✂ And I really need a poo

✂ Seriously, I need to go

Warmth

TOP 10
TAKING A DUMP

 #10 THE LITTER TRAY Stinks bad. Gets between your toes. Why not just let us shit outside?

 #9 GRASS You know the saying: 'Shit on grass, ain't got no class'. Don't do it. Grass is for filthy dogs.

 #8 THE PEOPLE TOILET This is only for those with a sense of irony.

 #7 THE BED Really pisses them off, but this could backfire when you need a warm place to sleep.

 #6 THE HIDDEN POO They will never know until the house goes on the market.

 #5 FOOT OF THE STAIRS For that slippery early morning surprise.

 #4 THE DECORATIVE GARDEN STONES You just have to christen them within a day.

 #3 THE BATH Under the flannel is best. Let's face it, that's not hygienic anyway.

 #2 SOIL That's more like it. You can hide your faeces in a wholesome, organic way.

#1
THE SLIPPERS
The ultimate insult and a cosy hidden place, to boot. It's got it all — privacy, sabotage and a bit of spite. Happy to be home now, sucker?

WRONG

MORE POOP SCOOP

If we need any more proof (and we probably don't, it's just that it's funny and there's nothing we like more than laughing at dogs), here's another picture of a stupid dog taking a huge dump in a public place (above). No humiliation is too great for a dog. Contrast this with Barney (below), snipping a loaf in his person's bath. It's private, it's discreet, but most importantly, it's very annoying for Barney's person. You go, Barney!

RIGHT

My Blanket®

KNOW YOUR PILLS

Do you have a problem with drugs? Of course you do! Welcome to *Pussy's* drop-in drug advisory centre. Together, we can stamp out this scourge

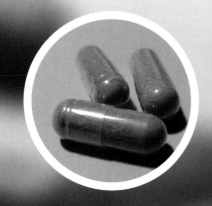

DRUG PROBLEM: They are smiling and trying to make you take a tablet.
SOLUTION: Ignore the tablet and purposefully mistake their attempts to coax you into taking it as an invitation to engage in some good-natured horseplay.

DRUG PROBLEM: They are looking serious and are trying to force a tablet down your throat.
SOLUTION: Use every muscle in your lithe and powerful feline body to fight them. Draw blood if necessary. Which it will be.

DRUG PROBLEM: They've wrapped your body in a towel with just your head popping out and are trying to force a tablet down your throat.
SOLUTION: Bite, close mouth, bite, close mouth.

Gob or ARSE?

Eye witness accounts from the front line of pill resistance...

BINKY
"My people tried to lace my grub with white powder. I punished them by refusing all food for days, until they desperately tried to feed me some very expensive smoked salmon. Now it's all I eat."

SOCKS
"I was relaxing in front of the fire one evening when my person came up and, without warning, grabbed me by the scruff and shoved a greasy pill up my arse. I've never been so humiliated. Oh, the shame."

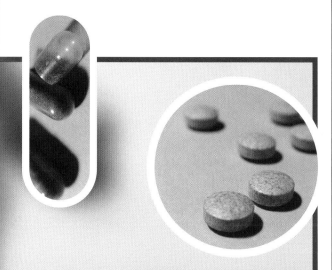

DRUG PROBLEM: They are arguing with each other, having become tetchy after your successful biting, and are wearing gloves. They have wrapped your body in a towel and are trying to force a tablet down your throat.
SOLUTION: Relax, look a bit sad and, when they drop their guard, try to scratch their eyes out.

DRUG PROBLEM: They're really angry with each other and a little scared of you. They are wearing eye protectors as well as gloves. They've wrapped your body in a towel and are trying to force a tablet down your throat.
SOLUTION: Go limp and feign death. When they panic (throwing down their gloves to pull off the eye protectors and unwrap the towel), run like bloody fuck. Hit the catflap at speed and stay out for three days.

DRUG PROBLEM: Having avoided all attempts at drug administration for weeks, you're feeling very ill.
SOLUTION: Lose weight, fall into a coma and wake up with parts of your body shaved, having undergone a series of life-theatening and expensive operations.

OSCAR (RIP)
"It's simple. Just look like you're swallowing the pill, then nonchalantly wander out through the catflap and spit it out. My person thinks I've been treated for worms when, in fact, I'm riddled with them."

WATCH OUT... THERE'S A DOG ABOUT

THE FUNNY SHAPES BOX

Our On The Box critic: Balfour

"*Television/Drug of the nation/Breeding ignorance/And feeding radiation…*"
So sang Michael Franti on The Disposable Heroes Of Hiphoprisy's seminal track, *Television*. But I think some stuff on The Funny Shapes Box is good. I love watching the coloured dots kicking the white dot around really fast while my person drinks stuff and swears. Sometimes he even cries. But sometimes he jumps about like an injured bird. I also like the afternoon stuff, with the adverts for awnings with that stupid dog Drummer. In the evening, I watch the animal stuff, and I like to see all the mating and killing. That's great. Hammy, my beady-eyed little co-habitee (he's too dangerous to be let out of his cage, of course), also watches The Funny Shapes Box. He likes the black and white stuff of people marching like geese and invading other people's territories. It makes him go crazy in his wheel.

DAMAGE

You've been hurting them and we're printing the pictures of the damage you've done. It's the article they tried to ban!

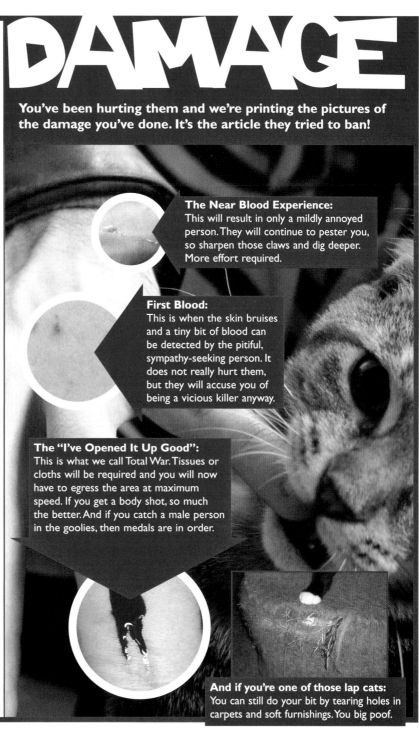

The Near Blood Experience:
This will result in only a mildly annoyed person. They will continue to pester you, so sharpen those claws and dig deeper. More effort required.

First Blood:
This is when the skin bruises and a tiny bit of blood can be detected by the pitiful, sympathy-seeking person. It does not really hurt them, but they will accuse you of being a vicious killer anyway.

The "I've Opened It Up Good":
This is what we call Total War. Tissues or cloths will be required and you will now have to egress the area at maximum speed. If you get a body shot, so much the better. And if you catch a male person in the goolies, then medals are in order.

And if you're one of those lap cats:
You can still do your bit by tearing holes in carpets and soft furnishings. You big poof.

Great Bins of Our Time

ROADSIDE RUMMAGING

Passing cars are a hazard, as anyone who remembers Julian (RIP) will tell you, but the pay-off can be huge. Ozzy once found the entire contents of an abandoned freezer, including six pounds of rancid pork, which he gorged himself on for a week.

WHEELIE (REGULAR & MAXI)

Also known as the Cat Trap, the Maxi Wheelie (left) is for the daredevil only. Often filled with water and rubble, it's rare to discover decent fish bounty. And if that lid shuts while you're in there, kiss another life goodbye.

STREET SURPRISE

Excellent for abandoned chicken 'dinners', which often taste like chicken, but also can be hazardous if approached by a person who smells of wee and shouts "Fark errrff pussy!" a lot.

DOMESTIC (ADVANCED)

In many ways, this is the classic. Knock the lid off at three in the morning and fill your boots. Voted Top Bin for 60 years on the trot. Don't eat the Hoover bags.

DOMESTIC (BEGINNERS)

Easy prey for the bin-lid shy, the bin bag can reveal a glorious bounty of stinky rubbish, and you can strew the mess all over the street. Another bonus is that it is likely to be blamed on foxes. Whatever they might be.

THE

TSIDER: MY DIARY

An occasional series in which cats with alternative lifestyles tell us about their lives. This issue, William discusses the pros and cons of being a 'house cat':

"Watching other cats prowling in my yard really rips my knitting. Watching birds taking the piss drives me insane. I can't bear the ming of my litter tray. I just can't stand it any more. What did I do to deserve this terrible torture? I despise the claustrophobia of my life. Help me to break out. There's a fish in it for you."

MY FAVOURITE BOOZER...

Coco (left): "The stone drinking fountain in the park serves a fine water, particularly on a hot summer's day, when there are dead bugs floating in it. Delightful."

Mindy (slightly less left): "I've yet to top the experience of sipping from the dripping tap in the sink. It's comfortable, homely and convenient. And unhygienic, of course."

THE TRUTH IS OUT THERE

PUSSY Stories Of The **PARANORMAL**

Case No.3: The Long Rabbits

Tuesday, 16:30hrs
For many days, Big Town has been buzzing with rumours about long rabbits. As kittens, we were told old stories under duvets late at night about these creatures. Long, wriggly, mutant offspring of floppy rabbits, long rabbits were supposedly foul-smelling, sharp-toothed and vicious. But could they be real?

Tuesday, 17:25hrs
Big Ginge from Number 37 goes missing.

Tuesday, 17:49hrs
Initial reports from our agents on the ground tell us Big Ginge had heard that some long rabbits were living in cages just behind the fishmonger's and set off to discover the truth. Foolish cat.

Tuesday, 21:05hrs
Little Tom turns up all excited and says he's found some markings on a nearby shed.

Tuesday, 21:12hrs
Looking at all of the arcane symbols and hieroglyphs on the shed, we deduce that they have been left by Big Ginge, and he appears to be telling us that he has located the long rabbits, and they are indeed the fearsome creatures of myth. We all tremble at the thought of poor old Big Ginge alone with these monsters.

Tuesday, 21:20hrs
There is one more thing that seems confusing about Big Ginge's final, desperate message: a scrawled image of a fish and an exclamation mark. We can only guess he was indicating exactly where the long rabbits lived, in a last-ditch attempt to warn us away for our own safety. Apparently they're near the bins at the back of the fishmonger's. We shall never go near the fishmonger's ever again, for that is the domain of the long rabbits.

Tuesday, 22:17hrs
Had some milk and went to bed.

Three weeks later, 09:45hrs
Little Tom says he's spotted a mystery cat who looks like Big Ginge, only he's twice as fat and smells of fish and burps a lot. What can this mystery sighting mean? Further investigation is required…

Big Ginge scrawled a last, desperate message on the shed: an arrow runs from a cat's eye to a frightening beast, and behind them is the international symbol for a fish – but what could it all mean?

Creammm

make time for cream
coming to a floor near you soon

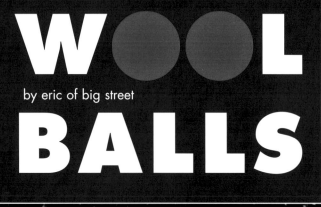

WOOL

by eric of big street

BALLS

THEY ARE OUT OF THIS WORLD!

FLUFFY I

Fluffy I arrived in Big Town on the *Mayflower* with the Pilgrim Fathers. They had left Other Town and pushed the boat over a mountain in the Jungle to get it here to Big Town. It took them seven months to cover the epic 400-yard journey. Today, the same trip takes a mere seven hours.

FLUFFY II

Fluffy II was the first of the Fluffy dynasty to be born in the newly founded Big Town. In the early days, Big Town was an anarchic hodge-podge of different cats from all over the world, and gang fights were common. Fluffy II wore a big top hat and was good at fighting. His gang, The Fluffies, established the town's first power elite, as immortalised in the film, *The Gangs Of Big Town*.

FLUFFY III

Shortly after the Gunpowder Plot (when those kids put a firework up Guy's jacksie), Fluffy III, Fluffy II's industrious and hard-working first-born, founded Big Town's first drop-in centre for fallen lady cats. He was later run out of town when it was discovered he'd been rogering each and every one of his poor and unfortunate charges.

FLUFFY IV

With a mother of loose moral character and a hypocritical philanthropist cat rogerer as a father, Fluffy IV was an angry young cat who died young: he got his tail caught in the sausage machine at the Gonk Manufacturing Co. He was the 963rd cat to die in that way.

FLUFFY V

Fluffy V became the richest cat in Big Town after investing in tuna. He spent his money on trying to build a flying machine that didn't work. He then lived in isolation and grew his claws really long and went mental, mental, chicken oriental.

FLUFFY VI

Also known as Churchill, Fluffy VI successfully led the Big Town army to victory when the evil hordes from Other Town tried to invade. "We shall fight them in the gardens, we shall fight them in the sheds, and in the morning, I will be sober," he famously said. A great military strategist, Fluffy VI also won the hearts of the population when he announced "Now I can look the East End in the face" after his palace got bombed.

FLUFFY VII

You know him as Fluffy. Shame he's such a twat.

FLUFFY'S FAMILY TREE

Until now, nobody has ever researched Fluffy VII's family tree. Until now, there has never been an exhaustive study made of the enormous Fluffy legacy. And until now, we weren't able to exclusively reveal the truth. Until now…

THE EMPTY DECORATIVE BOWL

Do they think we'd be more interested in this because it looks like a dog has walked all over it? Unbelievable.

CUDDLY TOYS

If we wanted to play with a small furry creature, we'd kill one.

THE TOP & TAIL WET WIPES

Just because they need toilet paper, they think we do, too. The sheer arrogance of their logic is astounding.

TOP & TAIL

Wipes

FOR LARGE ~~~~ ~~~~ PETS

POINT OF THAT, THEN?

THE PLASTIC POO SCOOPER

Is this really a dignified solution to a problem? What exactly is wrong with scraping soil over our turds?

THE MITTEN

What is it with kittens and mittens? When will they learn? WE DON'T WEAR ANY CLOTHES AT ALL.

TINS

Why? This is just cruel. We're clever, but not that fucking clever.

THE OVERLY SOPHISTICATED TOY MICE COLLECTION

Style over content, people.

THE LOCKABLE CATFLAP

You've been busy all night, you're shagged out, and you want warmth, food and peace. And they've locked the catflap. Great.

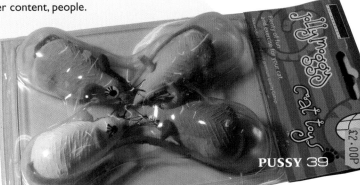

sky

There's always something worth watching

COMPETITIO

WIN! WIN! WIN! WIN! WIN! WIN

HOLIDAYS IN THE SUN!

NOT SEMI-SKIMMED!

IN! WIN!

SPECIAL MYSTERY PRIZE!

The prizes we have this issue are so good, we can scarcely believe it.

The top prize is an indefinite stay at the Big Town Cattery/Glue Works. This upmarket cattery promises luxury accommodation for you and as many members of your family as you would like to share your fabulous prize. And if you have any relatives or friends with particularly large pelts, just bring them along. No need to take anything with you, all food will be supplied, and they tell us that there's probably no point in letting anyone know where you're going, because the chances are you'll love it so much that you will never want to leave. They also told us not to worry about that gonk manufacturing controversy a few months ago. It was all lies, apparently.

If you're not lucky enough to bag our main prize, don't worry, because you'll still be in with a chance to win our relatively impressive second prize, which is a rummage inside the bin from Number 32. This bin has been the source of some amazing discoveries over the years – who could forget when Bingo found all those big crunchy insects in there, for example? They called it an infestation, we called it a banquet. Third prize is saucer of milk (Gold Top, yay!). OK, so third prize is a bit lame, but what are we, a frickin' charity?

To win, just answer the following question:

A gonk is made of…

a) Rabbit fur

b) Mouse fur

c) Some other kind of fur, but definitely not cat fur. That was just a rumour put around by a rival glue factory.

Answers to the usual address as soon as you like. The editor's decision is suspect.

TRUE LIFE
CONFESSIONS

"My Best Friend Was A Dog"

"I grew up in a normal home. There was nothing unusual about us. I pooed in a cat litter tray until I was three months old, played with empty cotton reels, ate, slept and tried to find my way in the world, just like any other kitten. And all through my kittenhood, there was Rover. I could rely on Rover, he was always there for me. When I fell, he would pick me up. When I was scared, he would comfort me.

"I didn't notice anything out of the ordinary about Rover. I mean, you don't when you're young, do you? It's only later when differences seem to become more important than the things which bind us all together. The world can be so cruel.

"I suppose the first time I realised that our relationship was considered something to be ashamed of, a sickness even, was when I was about nine months old. Rover and I were in the back garden. I was relaxing in the sun, watching Rover stand over the sprinkler with his ears pricked up, trying to bite the jets of water as they came up. He was always doing funny things like that. Then I noticed a couple of cats up on the garden fence. I recognised them as Miggins and Monty. I'd seen them around before and not thought much of it. We'd just ignored each other. But this time, it was different. They started shouting abuse – dreadful things about me and Rover. I was so humiliated. I pretended not to hear what they were saying, but I did. Although Rover chased them away, I could still hear their cruel laughter ringing in my ears for days afterwards.

"I saw the two cats again the following week. I was trying to walk along the garden fence when I spotted them. They were on the wall on the other side of next door's garden. We stared at each other for a long time, not moving. Then it started: 'Urgh! You like dogs!', 'Dogs smell! Hahaha!' and 'You freak!'.

The abuse came thick and fast. At one point, they told me I was a disgrace to feline kind and that what I was doing was

"You fucking freak!" they shouted...

diseased. I couldn't believe my ears. How could a friendship that was so happy and caring cause such hatred? Why should Rover and I be judged for our love?

"Rover and I talked it over that evening. He looked at the floor as I explained as best I could my feelings for him, and yet how impossible our situation seemed to be. It felt awful and wrong and frightful to be saying these things. Rover looked up, his eyes ablaze with passion. 'We don't have to take this,' he barked. 'We can fight back, we should be able to walk with our heads held high,' he went on. 'Yes!' I cried. 'Oh, Rover, what shall we do? How can we fight them?' I mewled, pitifully. 'With you by my side, I can do anything,' he cried, and I felt my aching heart would burst.

"The next day, I saw Rover in the garden. He had a strange smile playing across his lips. 'Those cats won't be bothering us any more,' he said as I walked towards him, a questioning look on my face. 'I chased them,' he said. 'And I caught them. Then I bit their fucking heads off.'

"I was stunned. Rover had killed our tormentors. We were safe at last. No more would we have to suffer the living hell of Miggins and Monty taking the piss. Rover had killed them. I wanted my revenge, too, but I'd just gone into their garden and done a shit under the rose bushes. Still, that's dogs for you, they do tend to get over-excited.

"Anyway, it turned out that Monty and Miggins lived with these people next door, and when they discovered the mangled corpses of the two cats, they came round and talked to our people for a while, and then Rover was taken off to the vets. I think they gave him a lethal injection or something. I haven't seen Rover since – and that was over a year ago now. Come to think of it, his name might not have been Rover. I can't really remember any more. I don't give a shit, to tell you the truth."

BEHIND
BLUE EYE

A full pedigree ragdoll, a blue-eyed babe and an all-round class act – Millie needs no introduction. Following her success at the Cat Show, we interview the pussy you're all talking about ▶

S

Can I start by asking you how your life has changed since you won the Cat Show?

Some things have certainly changed – I now sleep on a beautifully soft cushion and my person gives me fresh fish two or three times a week – but I'd like to think I still have my paws on the ground. I'm just Millie from the block, y'know. I love the fact that I get lots of attention in the street now, though.

Attention from tom cats, you mean?

Yeah. That's a real buzz for me. I've had it all my life, but not to this extent. Of course, I've always been a cutie – I didn't win the Cat Show for nothing, y'know. But you will still find me getting rogered senseless behind the fish shop when I'm in town. And on heat.

So what do you look for in a tom?

A sleek coat and strong hind quarters. Like every girl, I suppose! But while looks are important to me, feline-ality is also a factor. I've got brains as well as beauty. It takes more than a swishy tail and a swagger to impress me. I quite like older toms, actually. I like a tom who's been through a few lives. They know the score. That's a turn-on for me.

▶

What about grey whiskers? Are they a turn-on?

They can be. I don't like bald patches, though. I don't think that baldness is a sign of virility. I think it's just a sign of… well, the mange, mainly.

I've heard a rumour that you might be starring in a movie. Is that right?

There has been some talk of it, yes. I overheard my person on the dog 'n' bone the other night and, from what he was saying, I think he was talking to someone in Hollywood. He's had a video camera for ages and I thought he just used it to film lady persons' bottoms, but since my success at the Cat Show, he's started shooting footage of me. So far it's been simple stuff, *au naturel* shots of me walking around and sitting on the sofa, and I'm waiting for him to show me the script before I agree to it, but I'm very excited at the possibility.

Can I have sex with you now?

No.

Oh, go on.

All right then. But be quick, I've got an appointment with the flea doctor in 10 minutes.

JIM'S TIN ROOF

Girl cats free B4 11pm
Friday karaoke (all night)
Fighting (Saturdays only)
No collar, no entry

S HOT!

CATNIP!

It sends you round the bend, it does your head in and it mongs you out proper, but what's THE TRUTH about our fave herb?

Some catnip, yesterday

J asper (not his real name), a lean, four-year-old ginger tom, shifts his weight and gazes off into the middle distance. You wouldn't know it to look at him, but Jasper has a secret. He is a catnip addict. "I remember the first time I did catnip," he says, wistfully. "I didn't know what it was or what was happening to me. It started when my person brought out a toy mouse. I'd seen toy mice before and, y'know, they were all right, but I'd soon get bored with them and walk off. There was something different about this one, though. As soon as I batted it, something came over me. I lost it a bit. I saw colours in my head. I went a bit mad." ▶

In fact, Jasper had enjoyed his first trip, caused by the stuffing inside the mouse: a herb called catnip.

"After that, things escalated fast. My person came home with a bag of pure catnip and put a small pile of it on the floor. I went up to it, sniffed it… and that was it. I went totally fucking mental and nothing was going to stop me. You could have shoved a thermometer up my bum and I wouldn't have cared. It was that good. After running around for 10 minutes, rubbing my face in it, eating it, snorting it, I was totally fucked.

I couldn't be arsed to move and I slept for 19 hours in a single stretch. That's two hours more than usual."

Now, Jasper says, his life is completely dominated by catnip. "All I want to know is where the next lot of nip is coming from. Once, I found the bag and helped myself. I ate the lot and was sick as a dog. I shat my arse off, too. My person now hides it above the kitchen cupboard where I can't get it. Or so he thinks."

Jasper's experience of catnip is not unusual. But according to Sooty, secretary

of the More Catnip Now! campaign, we shouldn't allow scare stories to marginalise catnip users, many of whom suffer no ill-effects and do not develop an addiction.

"It is a contentious area, but there's no medical evidence to support the claim that catnip is addictive," says Sooty. "It is non-toxic and doesn't have any long-term side effects. Obviously, we don't recommend heavy catnip use – that is simply abusing the herb – but as a recreational drug, why not? It really isn't any more

Dr Benway's controversial third album

or less harmful than eating grass or running around in circles chasing a piece of string. It's good, harmless fun, and we believe that it can give you insights into feline existence."

Sitting in Sooty's bookcase is a well-pawed copy of *Catflaps Of Perception*, the counter-culture Bible by author Mogston O'Reilly. Written entirely under the influence of catnip, *Catflaps Of Perception* informs an entire generation of pussy drop-outs who eschew traditional cat pursuits like killing mice and birds, fighting, and sitting on window sills dozing off. Instead, these catnip activists propose a new way of life for cats, a way of life largely consisting of sleeping, expressing a disdain for human company

represents something of a departure for Dr Benway and his production team, The Pussy Posse.

"Wiv dis album, me wanna explore new directions, innit?" he slurs when we catch up with him backstage at The Cardboard Box, the venue in the East District alley where Dr Benway's fanbase is at its most ardent. Fat Cat and Notorious C.A.T., two key members of The Pussy Posse, nod in agreement. "Me did all me fighting and fucking tunes wiv de first elpee, den me did de sex rhymes wiv *Stroke Da Pussy*. But now me gets more conscious wiv *Catnip Trip*. It's about expansion of da mind, for all da feline kind, if you look you can find, a new way to lick your behind. Aiii."

Catnip has long played a part in the

"I went totally fucking mental and nothing was going to stop me"

and writing poetry.

"Why do we fight?" ponders Sooty. "Why do we kill? Why do we spray up against things with that peculiar tail-juddering motion? Are we nothing more than biological mechanisms mindlessly replicating behaviours taught us by our parents? Some of us are asking these difficult questions, and it's catnip that helps us step outside of ourselves and find a new framework to develop a fresh narrative for feline kind."

Sooty suddenly sticks his back leg in the air and licks his anus frantically for a few moments.

"If you want to find out about the catnip movement world-wide, check Dr Benway. He is the spokescat for the catnip generation. He knows what time it is."

Dr Benway, cat rap icon and catnip enthusiast, has just released his third album, *My Catnip Trip*. It comes hot on the heels of his previous two works: the shocking debut, *Fighting, Fucking*, and its follow-up, *Stroke Da Pussy*. *My Catnip Trip*

creation of Dr Benway's unique sound, but this album represents a shift from the street rhymes concerned with the dark underbelly of cat life in the East District, to a more enlightened approach, calling for cat unity and revolt against the controls he sees exerted by people.

This new approach is reflected in the crowds that Dr Benway is attracting. At previous shows, there have been a dozen maulings, countless ear bitings and one young cat lost his tail in a particularly vicious gang fight while Dr Benway was on stage performing his underground hit, *Fuck Da Siamese*.

"I saw all the fighting among me feline brothers and sisters and I thought, 'We need to *reee*-lax'. So me chomp me a mountain of catnip, I give it out to the crowds, everyone goes doolally for a few numbers, then they chill. And we crank out de ambient shit wiv de bass in your face, just in case, you're in da wrong place."

So what does Dr Benway make of the spectre of catnip addiction? ▶

STASH HUNT!

1) Stash is usually hidden up high. Approach with caution – slippery surfaces.

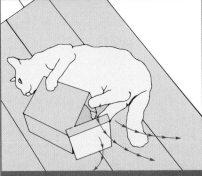

2) Clasp catnip container with front paws. Apply rapid disembowelling strokes.

3) Clean up after yourself – kids aren't mature enough to handle the hard stuff.

"Dat is propaganda," he says. "You cannot get addicted to da catnip. Catnip comes from the earth, it is a natural 'erb, given to us by the Great Cat. Watcha don' wanna do, is eat so much that you have to poo, like a volcano out your bum, an' puke like dog food, Chum."

Dr Benway's defence of catnip might seem irresponsible given the experience of users like Jasper, but it can't be denied that violence at his Cardboard Box shows has all but disappeared since he started distributing nip for free. Can we afford to condemn catnip when it seems to have such therapeutic benefits? And, after all, who can stand up and claim that he hasn't been off his trolley for hours at a time after a catnip binge?

Come on, we all do it. For example, I've just gobbled about a pound of the stuff while writing this article, and right now I'm starting to hallucinate like a spacecat. Oh man, I'm flying, I feel like I'm at one with the universe. Put on that Grateful Dead album, would you, man? I just want to groove on down to those beats. I'm just gonna sit down here quietly in the corner. Hehehehe. I was just thinking, d'you remember that TV programme? It was on in the 1970s. The one with all the frogs and elephants in it. They were made out of green stuff. Green stuff! Green elephants and then the thing happened with the other thing. Hehehehe. They must have been on catnip when they put that together. D'you remember the theme tune? 'Doo doo doo bap bap diddly wah wah.' It was ace! Great Cat, I'm hungry. Anyone got any toast? Hold on, what's going on here? Oh no, my person looks really angry. He's making one of those cigarettes with those Rizla things and his special bag is empty. Hehehe. He's going mental. Hehehe. That's the catnip I ate. Hehehe. I ate all his catnip. Oh dear. That wasn't catnip? What was it, then? I feel sick…

Help me, help me…
(That's enough nonsense - Ed)

The handy map of BIG TOWN

THE DRAIN pIpe

the Fish & Chip shop

The back Alley

Illegal catnip distribution routes through Big Town

CATNIP: THE FACTS

● Catwort, catrup, catfucker, stink – call it what you will – catnip is a plant from the mint family which includes *mintus polo, neverhurrya murray mintus* and *toothus pastus.*

● Catnip is grown in small plastic boxes which are kept in high places. Probably.

● The most catnip ever consumed by one cat in one sitting was by Syd. He ate his own body weight in catnip last Thursday. It might have been Wednesday, actually.

● Wozzer was banned from the sleep marathon in the last Cat Games when he was found to have taken catnip the night before. "We cannot condone deliberate monging," said the umpire, angrily.

● We get ours off Bender. Meet him by the drainpipe in the back alley – half a tin of Whiskas, a quick lick round the ears and Bob's yer uncle.

● Come to think of it, Syd's spectacular catnip session was on Tuesday.

The PET SHOP

no. 57

The pond

sum CATNIP

the VETTS???

Some alarming symptoms of catnip abuse, yesterday

**THINK ONCE
THINK TWICE
OH FUCK IT....**

JUST GO FOR IT!.

SLEEP

IS 18 HOURS A DAY REALLY ENOUGH?

Did you ever wonder where the expression 'catnap' comes from? No, of course you didn't – that's because you're a cat. However, there's a fine line between a catnap and a fully-fledged kip. One moment you're just resting your eyes, the next you've been deep in snoozeville for hours. Perhaps even days. But what exactly is sleep? And are we getting enough of it? Is there such a thing as too much sleep? Who cares? Just relax and lose consciousness with *Pussy's* guide to extreme torpor.

Pussy contributor Spangles researching this story, yesterday

Sleep expert Dr Sleep calls sleep "the periodic suspension of consciousness that is essential for physical and mental well-being". But he cribbed that out of the dictionary. He is a useless charlatan, really. He just goes about talking in a Viennese accent, saying things like, "Ah, yes, you haf ze lurgy und I recommend a veek in bed und much eating of the choccies and the like", and everyone goes, "Ooh, Dr Sleep, he's really great and knows all about being a doctor, which is pretty unusual considering he's a pussy cat, and he gave me some great advice when I was feeling a bit Uncle Bill after eating all those cockroaches", but he's not a doctor at all. What a knobhead. I hate him loads. *[Spangles, would you stop slagging off our expert doctor and get on with it – Ed]*

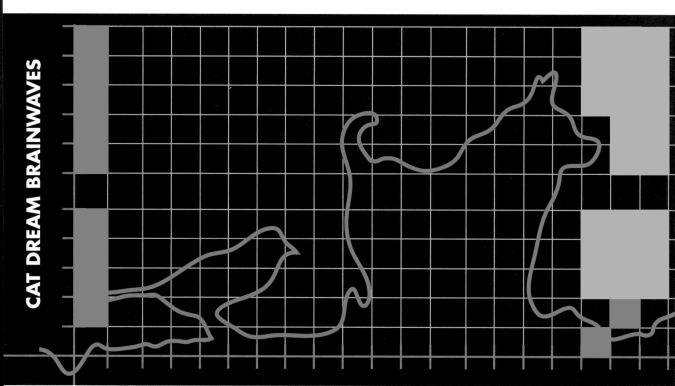

CAT DREAM BRAINWAVES

Dr Sleep takes up the story: "Ah yes, schleep. I vill try to put it in laycat language for your readers. Schleep is vary knickersary for de pussy cat. If ve do not schleep for ze 18 hours a day, ve vill find dat ve veel vary schleepy all da time and perhaps vill even run da risk of falling fast aschleep with our noses in da bowl with the food in, or verse, in da tray with the grit and the poopie in. And that's nicht nice."

Dr Sleep conducted the infamous sleep experiments at Stanford University in 1969. The tests were shut down when six cats got the screaming heebeegeebees after being subjected to three weeks of sleep deprivation with all electrodes and that stuck to their heads and Dr Sleep walking around going, "Nicht schleepen! Nicht schleepen!" in a really loud voice. However, despite the controversy surrounding the largely discredited clinical trials, the results of Wango The Supreme's brain wave scan (see below) have provided medical science with food for thought.

"As you can see," says Dr Sleep, placing a fat paw on the print-out, "firscht of all, it zeems that Wango The Supreme vas dreaming about ze small bird-like creature, possibly a robin or maybe a schparrow, but definitely nicht a pigeon or anyzing like dat. Shortly after, he has ein big scary dream about a dog. You can tell ze dream vas a big one because ze read-out at zis point in da schleep pattern becomes really quite exaggerated, with extreme peaks und troughs. Finally, Wango calms down and dreams about a mouse or a rat. Or it might be a gerbil or schomething along those lines."

Beyond Dr Sleep's useless experiments, more field work has been completed by an informal network of enthusiastic amateurs. Inspired by some of feline kind's more eminent sleepers, Jimmy, Dog The Cat, Splash and Kishi have been comparing notes on their own sleep patterns and have made some startling discoveries, as Jimmy outlines:

"My people came back from a shopping trip with an enormous package from the pet mart. They had bought a big comfy cat basket with a special cat blanket inside and the words 'Cat's Bed' written on the side. It must have cost a mint. They took it out of the large cardboard box and put it on the floor near the radiator, so I got into the cardboard box and fell asleep and ignored the cat basket. It was really comfy. I never did sleep in the cat basket." ▶

DREAM ON!

All that remains of Dr Sleep's highly controversial Stanford University sleep experiments of 1969 is this very small fragment of Wango The Supreme's brain wave scan. After years of analysis, Dr Sleep published his theory that Wango had been dreaming about birds, dogs and some kind of small rodent.

"You must ünterstant," Dr Sleep told *Pussy* when we approached him to ask him about the closure of the experiments and the removal of his funding, "dat ze people in charge, ze ones looking after ze money, are ignoramii with not an idea of how the schcientific community works to advance our knowledge for ze good of feline kind. For example, I am now in ze process of developing a mutant dog/cat/fish dat will be able to eat itschelf and run away from itschelf simultaneously. And they call me mad? Vot is wrong with you? Ach!"

As *Pussy* went to press, Dr Sleep was taken into custody and officials from the health authority closed down his clinic.

Nearly asleep (above) and out of it (below)

And according to Kishi, sleep is just great:

"Sleep is just great," she says. "I love it, me. There's no such thing as too much sleep. If I could, I wouldn't bother waking up. But sometimes I get hungry and need a poo. And sometimes I like running around really fast and hiding behind things and then jumping out suddenly. That's great. I love it, me."

So is there any reason why we should be concerned about the amount of sleeping we do? Does sleeping for 18 or even 20 hours out of every 24 pose any potential threat to our well-being? Are there any steps that we should take to minimise sleep-related risks? Obviously, you should avoid any of Dr Sleep's unofficial sleep experiments which are being held behind the shed at Number 53 (Alan has gone mental), and Dog The Cat has some words of warning for the unwary:

"Sleep is good for you, as long as you take certain precautions. For example, when you're inside, and you're sitting in front of the fire with the glass door in front of it, try not to nod off. You might accidentally press your nose against the glass while you're asleep and, believe me, that hurts like buggeration."

We here at *Pussy* recommend that you ignore Dog The Cat's opinions: he is a complete and utter moron. Sleep all you like and arse to the consequences. We've all got nine lives, so why not sleep for six of them?

That's what we say, anyway.
Night, night.
Zzzzzzzzzzzzzz.

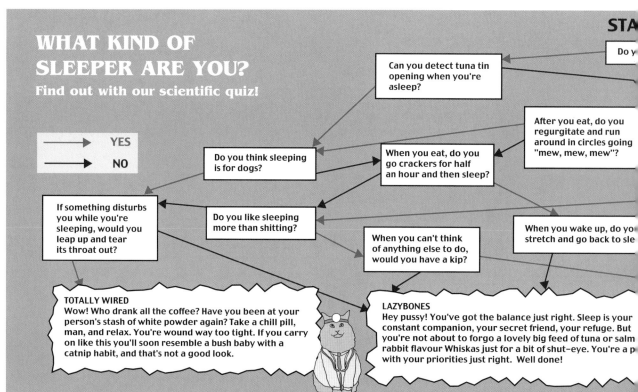

TOP SNOOZERS IN CAT HISTORY

• Grommity Spommity (daughter of Dommity Spommity) made sleep history when she fell asleep in the world cup itself when it was stolen in 1966 and abandoned under a bush. She was actually asleep in the cup when the stupid dog, Pickles, found the cup and alerted the authorities. While Pickles went on to world fame for finding the cup, pussy historians should note that it was a cat that found the cup first. It's just that she couldn't be arsed to let anyone know and was feeling a bit sleepy at the time.

• Eric, also known as The Viking, once slept solidly for 10 days, without even waking up briefly to suddenly lick his front legs, after coming across an entire salmon which he ate in just over an hour. He was so soundly kipped out that his people thought he was dead and took him to the vet in Main Street. The vet discovered that he wasn't actually brown bread, but put him on a life support system just in case. When Eric finally woke up, he did the largest poo ever recorded in Big Town, making Eric The Viking a double record breaker and a legend in *Pussy*'s opinion. He got squashed by a car in 1986.

• Sleepy Simon is still fast asleep in a milk crate down by the river. He's been asleep in there now for well over three months, and crowds continue to gather to cheer him on. And chuck things at him, too. However, rumours that he is faking it, and goes out for food and to wee when no one's looking, are starting to undermine his celebrity status.

• *Pussy*'s staff writer Spangles, who joined us from *It Smells* magazine last year, is the most prolific sleeper in the office. Only last week he left the office saying he was "just popping out for a sandwich and a cup of coffee", and offered to bring back back a cream cheese and salmon bagel for the editor, only to be found four days later snoozing in the cardboard box under the photocopier where we keep the envelopes. He is actually sound asleep while he is writing this feature and is about to be sacked for his naked incompetence.

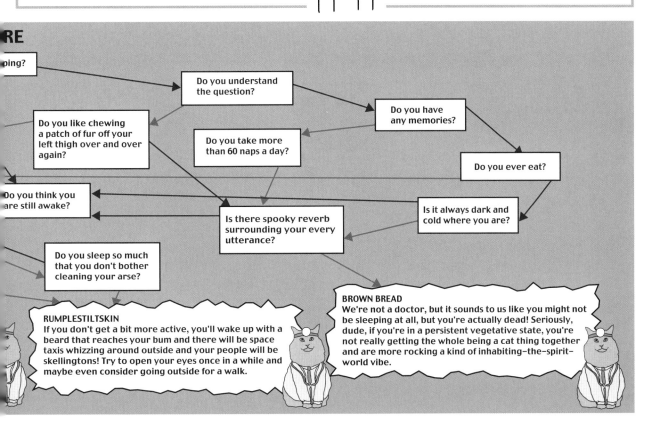

RE

ping?

Do you understand the question?

Do you have any memories?

Do you like chewing a patch of fur off your left thigh over and over again?

Do you take more than 60 naps a day?

Do you ever eat?

Do you think you are still awake?

Is there spooky reverb surrounding your every utterance?

Is it always dark and cold where you are?

Do you sleep so much that you don't bother cleaning your arse?

RUMPLESTILTSKIN
If you don't get a bit more active, you'll wake up with a beard that reaches your bum and there will be space taxis whizzing around outside and your people will be skellingtons! Try to open your eyes once in a while and maybe even consider going outside for a walk.

BROWN BREAD
We're not a doctor, but it sounds to us like you might not be sleeping at all, but you're actually dead! Seriously, dude, if you're in a persistent vegetative state, you're not really getting the whole being a cat thing together and are more rocking a kind of inhabiting–the–spirit–world vibe.

SPOOKY TWINS

The cat on the left is called Mercury. The cat on the right is called Saturn. No, wait, Saturn is on the left. Erm, no, hold on a minute… We're in deep double trouble here. Welcome to the Twilight Zone. Twice ▶

SPOOKY TWINS

Can I first ask who is Saturn and who is Mercury?
Saturn: I'm Saturn.
Mercury: No, you're not. I'm Saturn.
Saturn: No, no, no. I'm definitely Saturn.
Mercury: Are you sure?
Saturn: Well, now you come to mention it...
Don't you know who is who?
Mercury: Of course!
Saturn: I'm Mercury...
Mercury: Look, how many more times have I got to tell you? You are not Mercury. I am Mercury. You are Saturn.
Saturn: Are you sure?
Mercury: Well, now you come to mention it...

Have you always been confused?
Mercury: About what?
About who's who?
Saturn: Whose what?
Have you always been confused about who's who?
Saturn: We're not confused. It's you that's confused.
Mercury: It's probably because you keep moving, Mercury.
Saturn: I'm not moving. It's you that keeps moving.
Mercury: No it's not. It's you. First you're on one side of me, then you're on the other...
I don't think either of you were moving, actually...
Saturn: [*to interviewer*] It must be you, then.
Mercury: Yeah, it must be you. Someone keeps moving and it isn't

PUSSY 71

JUST SAY NO

me. And it isn't Mercury. So it must be you.

Maybe we should press on. You have a reputation for being a bit spooky...

Mercury: I'm not really that spooky. Mercury's the spooky one. Aren't you?

Saturn: Me? ME? Are you talking about me? I keep telling you, I'm not Mercury. I'm Saturn.

Mercury: Oh. Right. Saturn's the spooky one, then.

Saturn: Make your mind up, will you. You just said Mercury's the spooky one.

Mercury: No I didn't. I said you were the spooky one. Didn't I say she was the spooky one?

You did say that, but...

Mercury: See. Now will you stop confusing me... ▶

BECAUSE WE KNOW YOU CAN'T ASK FOR IT YOURSELF

Saturn: Sorry, Saturn.
Mercury: I'M NOT SATURN. I'M MERCURY.
Saturn: You're not, not, not. NOT! I'M MERCURY.
Maybe we should try to move on...
Mercury: Why do we have to go through this all the time, Saturn? It's always the same with you. It's just soooo boring. You're a fucking arse, you are.
Saturn: I'm not a fucking arse. You're a fucking arse.
Well, I must say it's been fascinating talking to you. Most of the models that we speak to have nothing to say, but interviewing you has been an unforgettable experience. I'm afraid we're almost out of time, but is there anything you'd like to add before we have to end?
Mercury: We are Siamese if you please.
Saturn: We are Siamese if you don't please.

FeRAL

Sure, you sit around and boast about your genetically inherited hunting skills but, seriously, when was the last time you actually killed anything? Going out and finding a mouse that was already dead doesn't count. Have you forgotten your roots? Can you still run with the pussy posse? Think you can? Well, so do we, which is why we went to meet the hardest pussies of them all. And we got more than we bargained for...

KULTURE

Countryside killing machine?

MORRIE THE WIG
Don't mention the wig

FREDDIE NO NOSE
Don't mention the nose

SHINY MAC
Likes violence and chasing butterflies

TOMMY
Can you hear me?

JIMMY TWO TIMES
"I gotta go get the tuna, get the tuna"

FRANKIE
Says relax

Big Farm. Most cats would give the place a wide berth. Real danger lurks in every corner of this run-down part of town. In the agricultural hinterland, where the rules of the jungle persist, it's kill or be killed, and the cats that live here like it that way. We arrived at five in the afternoon in search of a true killer, and met a ginger and white bruiser who called himself Farmy.

His fur was coarse and matted. His feet were caked in mud and one eye was slightly closed from an injury sustained several years ago, fighting with a fox. But he told us he doesn't like to talk about it. Although he did:

"If any mo'fo comes into my patch, they get rubbed out," he snarled. "If a cat's gonna survive, you've gotta know how to fight. I don't like to talk about that night," he said. "I was walking around the place as normal. It was late, perhaps three in the morning. I thought that I heard something on my territory and I thought to myself, 'There's some mo'fo on my patch', so I went to investigate. I could see a figure moving about by the bins just outside the kitchen. Goddamn mo'fo. I pressed up against a wall and I got closer. It was a goddamn fox, helping itself to a chicken carcass. Mo'fo. So I stalked right up to it, and I leapt at its head and wrapped myself around it. But it took a cowardly swipe across my face before it ran off. Mo'fo. And that's how I got this," and he indicated his sort of Thom Yorkey squinty face eye thing.

"Yep," Farmy continued, and rolled over and showed his not inconsiderable belly with his back legs sticking in the air but his front paws tucked over his chest like a great big baby, "I'm a very tough cat."

Then we heard a noise in the near-distance. Farmy flipped over and, with some difficulty it has to be said, stood up. His ears were pointing towards the noise and his eyes were large and black.

"What is it, Farmy?" I asked him, quietly.

"I think it's…" said Farmy, slowly and deliberately, then we heard a person voice, high and soppy, and the rattle of a fork against a tin. I detected a slight whiff of Whiskas (tuna) in the air. The voice called out again: "Tinklebooby! Tinklebooby!"

"Tinklebooby?" I looked at Farmy in disbelief. "*Tinklebooby*?"

"It's tea-time. I'm off," he yelped, and then I'm sure I heard him say, "Coming, Mummy!" as he darted away. So, 'Farmy' turned out to be an overweight lap cat who answers to the name Tinklebooby. But our search for country toughnuts was about to take a far more sinister turn.

"Did he tell you he got that gammy eye from fighting a fox?" a voice hissed from the shadows. "Don't believe a word of it. He's just got an infection. He's on pills from the vet. They push them up his arse twice a day." From out of the foliage stepped a figure. He was thin. You could see his ribs under his fur. But he was muscular, tensed and ready to spring. He looked mean. "They call me ▶

Jimmy Two Times," he said. "Listen. Tinklebooby is a knobhead and a poof. A knobhead and a poof. If you want to know what it's really like around here, talk to me. You talk to me." Smudge, *Pussy*'s brave, award-winning photographer, tried to lift his Snappy CatCam® up to take Jimmy Two Times's picture.

"Take my picture and I'll push that Snappy CatCam® down your throat, mush," growled Jimmy. He sounded deadly serious, so Smudge let the camera dangle at his collar. We told Jimmy we had come to talk to a real country cat, a violent killer, but all we'd found was a fat old tart who goes crawling to people like some kind of slobbering, eager-to-please dog. Jimmy beckoned us into

the shadows and whispered into our ears: "You want to meet killers? I'll show you killers, kids."

Nervously, we followed Jimmy Two Times away from the main farm building. Then we ducked through a small hole in a wall and into a clearing in the woods. And there they were: Freddie No Nose, Frankie, Shiny Mac, Tommy and Morrie The Wig, slouching around in their gang den. It was terrifying. I did three plops very quickly. Smudge was paralysed with fear, but I grabbed his Snappy CatCam® and whipped off a few shots of the feral mob.

"So," growled the gang's leader, Freddie No Nose, "you come here, to my home, on my daughter's wedding day, and you show ▶

Tinklebooby: what a bullshitter

Dead Rabbits

*they're rabbits
and they're dead*

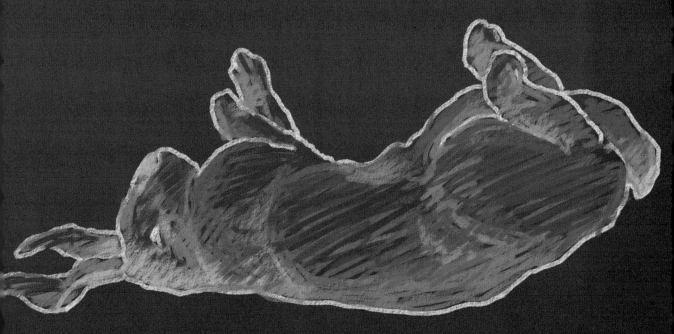

This product may contain traces of nuts, berries, carrots, lettuce and other vegetables

Morrie The Wig, just before he hit our correspondent

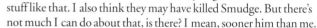

Tinklebooby gets carried away

me no respect? You disrespect me?", and it was then that Morrie The Wig hit me on my nose.

Smudge couldn't speak – and it was then I made my decision. I bloody legged it. Within three seconds, I was back through the hole in the wall and scarpering full pelt down the lane to Big Town.

So what did I learn from my encounter with our violent country cousins? I have certainly come away with a respect for the life of the feral gangs. They are self-sufficient and, unlike us town cats and the likes of Tinklebooby, they have rejected the cosy life of the mainstream pussy. They have a strict code of honour, where you should show some respect to Freddie No Nose on his daughter's wedding day or you get hit on the nose and stuff like that. I also think they may have killed Smudge. But there's not much I can do about that, is there? I mean, sooner him than me.

Next issue: Fraggles goes parachuting with the RAF

PUSSY'S GUIDE TO FERAL CHIC

Freddy No Nose and his gang of country cats are a collection of misfits and loons who really ought to have a good long look at themselves and sort it out. However, their feral style has been impressing the younger town cats around, erm, town. So, if you want to emulate the latest look, *Pussy* presents a guide to getting it without the violence! Or with it! Either way, if you want to look like a scabby old stray and frighten old ladies and dogs, here's a guide...

1) Don't clean your eye bogeys. Just let them run free. Cleaning eye bogeys is a requirement of The Man. Fuck them! You won't do what they tell you!

2) Don't clean your arse properly. 'Nuff said.

3) Get your ear all mangled. You can get it caught on the razor wire that mad old Mr Jenkins at Number 12 has put up around his house to stop people stealing his bicycle. You can pick a fight with Bouncer if you really fancy it. Or you could go to the Charlene's Nail Me beauty parlour (which is round the back of the arches) and have a nick taken out of your lug by a professional. It's very nearly painless and hardly any cats have died from the procedure

which, it has to be said, does involve a rusty lid off an old tin of tuna.

4) When it rains outside and there's lots of filthy mud everywhere, don't stay in dozing off in front of the gas fire until you accidentally touch it with your nose and have to hide under the bed to get over the pain and humiliation. Go out and sit in the mud. This is particularly effective if you're a long-haired breed.

5) Develop the mange. Just worry excessively about something until your fur starts falling out, then get in a really bad mood about it and stay in that bad mood all the time.

The new book by the acclaimed scientist Dr Sleep

DE-STRESS
A GUIDE TO MODERN LIVING

Dr Sleep RAC, NCP

"I found this book to be almost entirely useless" - Mogston O'Reilly (Author of *Catflaps Of Perception*)

"What book?" - Dr Benway

FUR cough publishing

THE FACE

"We knew it was a dog... It was too large for a cat ar

OF EVIL

t smelled of Bonio"

It was a bright summer's day in 1995 when Felix decided to go for a walk. He'd emerged from a catnap at midday and listlessly knocked around a cotton reel on the lino floor of the kitchen for a while. The night before had been nothing out of the ordinary, either. Felix had patrolled his territory for a few hours, had a playful spat with Blackie from Number 47, and spent half an hour sitting on the fence that separated Mr Patel's rambling garden from the neat, flower-bordered strip of land backing on to the house of the nice couple who often left half-full tins of tuna in their bin.

Yawning, Felix stepped through the kitchen door – always left open during the warm months – and sat licking himself on the back step for five minutes or so, before slipping under the gap in the fence. It was the last time he was seen alive. There was concern when he failed to return home, but nobody raised the alarm. Felix was an adventurous sort who would often stay out for extended periods without letting anyone know where he was.

Piecing together his lifestyle in the aftermath of his mysterious disappearance, detectives discovered that Felix led a seedy double life. He would frequent alleys and walk-ups around the red light district. He was known to receive bowls of milk and random acts of meaningless affection from the prostitutes plying their trade. On Friday and Saturday nights, he would also beg ▶

The murder spree ranged over three square miles. Inset: The location of the notorious Babes In The Tube murders

for winkles, cockles, and perhaps even cheese and onion crisps from the rough people frequenting the drinking dens. His appetites were, it appeared, depraved. All this came as a shock to his seven kittens, who had no inkling that their father, apparently a docile family cat who liked nothing more than three meals and 18 hours' sleep a day, was actually concealing another identity and a sleazy lifestyle.

More than one hypothesis for Felix's disappearance was explored by the police. Had Felix landed himself in debt trouble in the gambling dens? Or perhaps he'd been sleeping with the wrong girl cat and found himself on the receiving end of a gangland-style slaying? The police were in the middle of extensive enquiries into the catnip smuggling underground when they were suddenly called to a multiple murder three streets away from Felix's home. And this

time there was evidence – all too gruesome evidence – of a horrible murder.

"I thought I was gonna hurl when I first arrived at the scene," says Tiddles, investigating officer of the now notorious Babes In The Tube murders. Tiddles has since retired, his grey fur a testament to the eight years he spent investigating homicide for the Pussy Police. When Tiddles slipped through the wooden fence surrounding a three-acre stretch of wasteland down by the railway line, he came across a large concrete tube. He knew there was a family of

vagrant cats living in the tube – three kittens and a single mother. Family life was blighted by poverty and Officer Tiddles would visit every few days to make sure the young mother was coping. So when the call came through to HQ, Tiddles knew who the helpless victims would be.

"It was such a senseless waste," he recalls, bitterly. "I can remember seeing one paw hanging out of the tube, dried blood caked in the fur. As I got closer, the place was awash with blood and I could see that one of the kittens had a paw missing – it had been bitten clean off. The mother was nowhere to be seen, but the bloody remains of the three kittens were scattered around. They'd been torn apart. It was like something out of a horror movie."

Tiddles is visibly shaken as he recalls that night 10 years ago, and this from the puddy tat who broke up the cat-skinning operation of 1997, tracing it back to the local fairground's gonk manufacturing scam, and solved the Drowned Kittens In A Bag murders the next year.

"The job has hardened me up, but that first multiple murder hit me badly," says Tiddles. Indeed, after the six-month investigation and the mounting body count, Officer Tiddles had to go on compassionate leave for three months, and was often seen howling round the back of The Right Plaice, the local fish and chip shop. "I was in a bad way back there for a while," Tiddles confesses. "I was copping a lot of heat from City Hall, and I hit the catnip hard."

The body of the mother was found on the other side of the wasteland. She had

Officer Tiddles: "I was in a bad way back there"

clearly put up a desperate fight to protect herself and her kittens, but in the end had succumbed to a vicious killer. And then the police found the dismembered corpse of Felix. They deduced that Felix had been visiting the kittens' mother for some months, and may even have fathered one of the kittens himself. But the killer had left one clue: a coiled turd was found near the scene. "We knew it was dog," says Tiddles. "It was too large for a cat and it smelled of Bonio. And another dog came along and ate it, and we all know that dogs are forever eating each other's poo."

But one poo clue wasn't enough to make a positive ID and, over a tense summer, several more cats went missing and the body count steadily rose. One steamy evening, a small black cat known locally as Mini Ha-Ha was found dead. The next day, Sparkie (aka The Fat Persian) disappeared. His body was never found. And so it went on. Officer Tiddles was feeling the stress as the Mayor put the pressure on.

"Goddamn bureaucats," snarls Tiddles. "All they cared about was the next election and saving their own worthless hides. It was me on the front line – and they didn't like my methods. They were all worried about the rights of the criminal. Well, I'm all cut up about his rights…"

Tiddles was even the subject of an investigation himself, after being accused of harassment by a sausage dog called Slipper. Who can forget the image of Slipper, his face cut and bruised, yelping, "Officer Tiddles – he did this to me"? The investigation and the bad publicity was an unwelcome distraction from the real issue – out there somewhere was a vicious and remorseless killer who would, Tiddles had no doubt, strike again.

One day, Officer Tiddles made a routine call on one his informants, known only as Dog X. Dog X, in return for a discarded ice cream container (raspberry ripple) with ants crawling in it, showed Tiddles to a kennel, and it was there that Tiddles knew he'd tracked down his killer canine. The kennel belonged to a lurcher called Spike.

Spike was like any other puppy when he was growing up in the suburban sprawl of Big Town. He was affable and eager to please, happiest when chasing sticks thrown by his person. But Spike was developing murderous tendencies even back then.

The savagery with which he decimated his person's daily newspaper as it came through the letterbox alarmed the authorities, and Spike was sent to a ▶

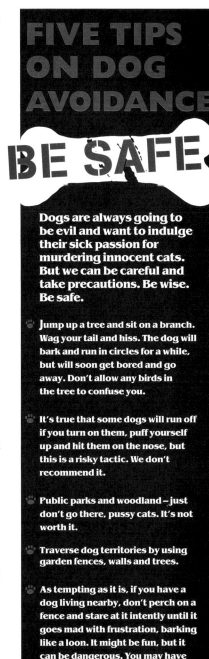

FIVE TIPS ON DOG AVOIDANCE

BE SAFE

Dogs are always going to be evil and want to indulge their sick passion for murdering innocent cats. But we can be careful and take precautions. Be wise. Be safe.

Jump up a tree and sit on a branch. Wag your tail and hiss. The dog will bark and run in circles for a while, but will soon get bored and go away. Don't allow any birds in the tree to confuse you.

It's true that some dogs will run off if you turn on them, puff yourself up and hit them on the nose, but this is a risky tactic. We don't recommend it.

Public parks and woodland – just don't go there, pussy cats. It's not worth it.

Traverse dog territories by using garden fences, walls and trees.

As tempting as it is, if you have a dog living nearby, don't perch on a fence and stare at it intently until it goes mad with frustration, barking like a loon. It might be fun, but it can be dangerous. You may have nine lives, but why risk any of them needlessly? Never forget: dogs are all evil and want to kill you.

CCTV footage (right) appeared to back up the police theory that a dog had been seen lurking around suspiciously fairly close to where the kittens, their mother and Felix were found. When analysed by forensics officers, it was concluded that the dog in the picture was probably Spike, the lurcher who lived in the kennel out by the gasworks who everyone hated cos of all the barking and stuff, even though Spike was a different colour to the dog captured on film.

"To be honest, we weren't all that bothered whether Spike had done it or not," says Bingo, the then head of the forensics laboratory. "We just made a couple of guesses that it probably was Spike and told Officer Tiddles to get on with it. He'd made up all the evidence anyway, so he didn't mind. If I remember rightly, we spent most of the rest of that day chasing a piece of string around the legs of a chair."

psychologist. It was discovered that he'd once done a poo behind the television in the front room, and his person had mercilessly rubbed his nose in it. It could well be this traumatic incident which set Spike on the path from happy-go-lucky stupid pup to an adult dog with psychopathic tendencies and an insatiable need to slaughter innocent pussy cats.

When Tiddles looked inside Spike's kennel, he saw that it had become a shrine to his twisted urges. The walls were covered with newspaper cuttings from the *Big Town Advertiser* (a story about the fire at the Cat Sanctuary had the words 'Arf Arf' scrawled across it in lipstick), and several hand-made lost cat posters, offering rewards under black and white photos of the lost cats, had been torn down from lamposts and lovingly added to Spike's sick altar of death. But the clinching piece of evidence was found under his dog blanket: a pussy cat paw. It obviously came from one of the poor kittens found in the concrete tube – and DNA tests soon confirmed that the paw belonged to Kitty Witty, the youngest of the litter who had had a bright future in purring ahead of her.

Spike was arrested and taken in an armoured vehicle to the Dog Sanctuary/ Crematorium. After three weeks in captivity, he was put down by lethal injection and his remains were buried in an unmarked grave. He was the most prolific

serial killer in cat history, confessing to no fewer than 48 pussy murders while he was in custody.

Sadly, Spike's notoriety has made him something of a celebrity among directionless young dogs looking for a transgressive anti-hero to worship, and many websites have sprung up celebrating his outsider status and crimes. The worry is that these will inspire a wave of copydog crimes by weak-minded canines who go around barking like bastards and causing mayhem all over the shop. There have been some attacks which have been blamed on the publicity given to Spike's murders, notably the spate of postman bitings of 1999, when four postmen had their ankles bitten by unknown assailants. Although never caught, the attackers were also suspected to have been responsible for the 'Spike Barmy Army' graffiti which sprung up around the same time. As we go to press, fears are mounting that the planned TV movie, *Spikey – Summer Of Fear*, may spark further violence. We can only hope that Spike's unhappy demise will serve as a warning for any dog harbouring aggressive intentions.

Perhaps the last word should go to retired investigating officer Tiddles: "There's a fairly strong chance that Spike didn't kill those kittens, because I fabricated the evidence, but one less dog in Big Town is good for all of us, isn't it?" Amen to that.

Spike being led to his drug-assisted death

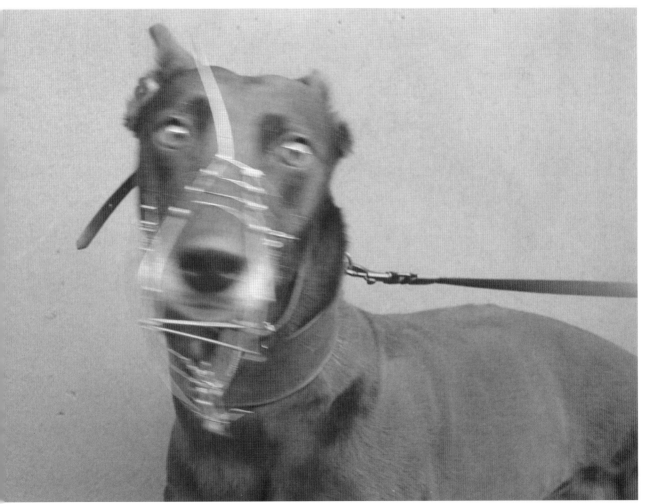

I WISH I WAS IN
DiXie

The southern belle from
across the big pond
has got the local toms
whooping. But is this
furry little charmer quite
what they think she is?

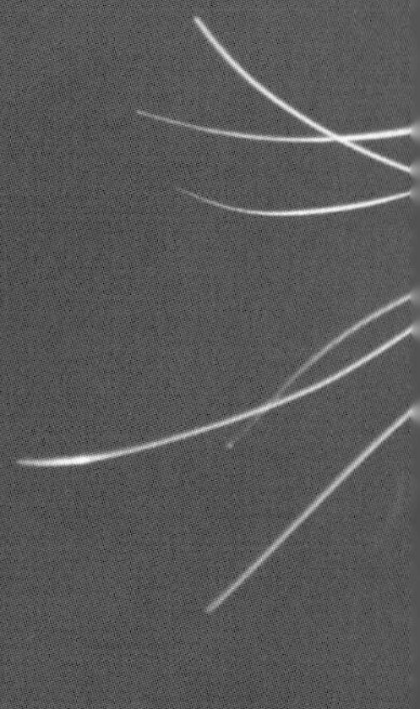

You're fairly new around here, aren't you?
That's right, honey. I was sitting on my satin cushion
one day, and the next thing I knew I was inside a golden
carrying case. I guess I must have been given a shot or
something. And I was in that golden carrying case for a
long time, honey. Mmm-hmm. I had to go all the way
across the big pond to get here.
Is it very different here to what you've been used to?
Yes it is. You know, where I come from, there wasn't a
single day when I didn't hear, 'Frankly my dear, I don't
give a damn.' For a lady like me, that was soooo
romantic. It was beautiful. But then there are some
beautiful things about this place as well. ▶

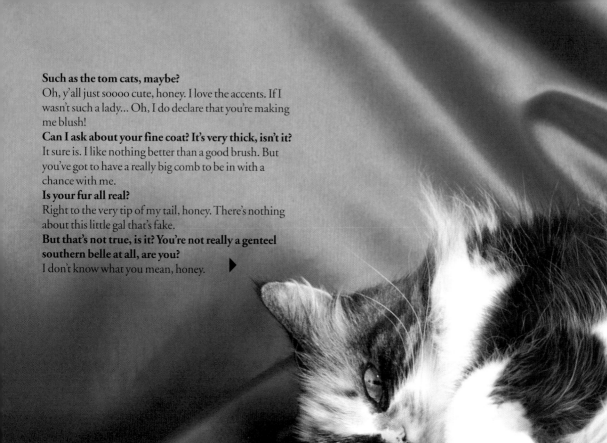

Such as the tom cats, maybe?
Oh, y'all just soooo cute, honey. I love the accents. If I wasn't such a lady... Oh, I do declare that you're making me blush!

Can I ask about your fine coat? It's very thick, isn't it?
It sure is. I like nothing better than a good brush. But you've got to have a really big comb to be in with a chance with me.

Is your fur all real?
Right to the very tip of my tail, honey. There's nothing about this little gal that's fake.

But that's not true, is it? You're not really a genteel southern belle at all, are you?
I don't know what you mean, honey. ▶

Well, we've heard that you don't come from quite as far away as you'd like everyone to believe...

Goodness gracious! What can you mean?

We've heard that you were carried here in a cardboard box from the other side of Big Town...

Lordy! I really don't know where you've got such a silly idea from.

Millie told us, actually.

Millie! Well, I do declare. She's a little minx, isn't she?

Yeah. She is. And she says the only reason you're called Dixie is because you used to live in the flat above that Kentucky Fried Chicken place...

Bollocks. Right, well, that's enough of this shite. Stick it up your arse, you fucking wanker. I'm off to find that bitch Millie...

SPORT

SMACK DOWN!

SHOCKING VIOLENT FIGHTING SHOCKER

FRED v TIGGY
THE HALLWAY, LAST THURSDAY

Violence! Get in!

It was everything we could have possibly wanted from a grudge match. The last time that these two met, it was over before it had started. One scratch, two bites and a yelp, and Tiggy the all-in wrestler had Fred the south paw boxer floundering on his back.

But this time, against the odds, it went the distance – the full 30 seconds. And what an astonishing 30 seconds it was. Even poor old Harold, who was on his way to the litter tray for the third time in an hour, nearly got pulled into the action.

This much-hyped re-match for the coveted Lonsdale Collar was a vicious battle from the off. Tiggy, as befitting his nickname of The Tiger, went straight for Fred's ears, pinning him down by squatting on his back and gnawing furiously on the hairy flaps. When Fred managed to flip over, they tumbled down the hallway in a blur of legs and tails.

Once they parted, Tiggy's claws came out, but Fred was too quick for him. A vicious jab caught Tiggy in his right eye. Stunned by the power of the blow, he struggled to stay on his four feet. A groan went up from the crowd. "That's one in the eye of The Tiger," someone muttered.

Fred went in for the finish. He sensed blood. A left, right, left combination had Tiggy rocking back on his haunches. A frenzied string of rabbit punches put him on the run.

"I done him good, Harry," a jubilant Fred told Harold as his battered opponent hid round the back of the sofa. "I'm the daddy now. Erm, has anyone seen my favourite mousey-wousey toy?"

Fred: "I done him good"

PUSSY 97

SHOCKING FOOTBALL VIOLENCE SHOCKER

Taisha took a run out on the park last weekend and the result was a vindication for Big Town's caretaker manager Royalty Violence. "I thought she was ready for a full match," said Roy. "Rumours that she's nothing more than a thug looking for opportunities to chew heads off and wreck everything in her path have turned out to be entirely accurate." Taisha's unspeakable savagery in the second half was matched only by her monstrous behaviour at the break, when she sicked up fish in the penalty area.

"You dirty northern bastards"

"You're gonna get your fucking head kicked in"

"You're shit…"

"You only sing when you're winning"

"The referee's a wanker"

Spot the cat

"She fell over, she fell over"

"…aaaaaahhhhhhhhhhhhrrrrrrrrgggggggghhhhhhhhhhhh"

"Zzzzzzzzzzzzzzzzzzzzzzzzzzzzzzzzzzz"

WINTER OLYMPICS MEMORIES

by Marvin, Big Town Olympic Champion

The Winter Olympics. If we're not training for them, we are thinking about them. As you know, I won three gold medals once. But like many Olympians, I'm modest about my awesome achievements. They are, after all, in the past. Where they tower over the puny attempts of today.

This year's Olympic squad is shaping up well. Spot is achieving personal bests in the Christmas Tree Felling Dash. We need a powerful pull-down for the last few baubles, and Spot has got strength and the right amount of disregard for his own safety. However, he won't touch my record of six baubles, plus damage to the Funny Shapes Box in the corner of the room (late Christmas Eve, no chance of getting it mended).

Meanwhile, Jones is impressing selectors with his Chewing Through The Christmas Lights skills, but they are all agreed that I was best at it and no cat has got the resilience to electric shock like what I had. And although Mr Muck's Christmas Pressie Wrecking is fast, he lacks the finesse for which I was famous.

And that's how I won my three gold medals. I'm great, me.

THE WORLD IS YOUR OYSTER

The world (right) is your oyster, and our award-winning travel correspondent Ratter helps you avoid the grit and food poisoning in his award-winningly wry and amusing manner, which many readers may find irritatingly smug, yet compelling, in a winning-of-awards kind of way...

There are few moments more satisfying than when you awake to find yourself bathed in glorious sunlight, streaming down from a different sky. *Tant pis!*

"Ah," you whisper to yourself as your eyelids gradually open and you take in the fresh scenery, "now I'm really travelling. *Nous aimons les jambons, n'est pas?*" The thrill of a change in atmosphere from one side of the fence to the other is enough to massage away the stress of the journey you have just undertaken in order to arrive at your chosen paradise. The weeks and months of daily slog you endured before you chose to move on melt away in one sublime moment of oneness with your environment. Travel, truly, is the balm of the soul. *Mais oui, mon capitaine…*

All of which is very well, I hear you cry, but where should we visit, and how do we get there avoiding the dog kennel at Number 45? *Comment allez vous?*

Well, *la plume de ma tante*, I've been all over the world, I've left every place, and I know where to be seen this year. *Par example*, you wouldn't want to find yourself at the *Côte du Piss*. Not when it's hot, anyway. *Salut! Ich bin ein Berliner!*

La Shed Avec Deux Green Doors, Le Next Door Jardin
The Shed With Two Green Doors has always held a mystical lure for the travelling pussy cat. You should thoroughly investigate this delightful tiny *shed de coal*, not forgetting to enjoy the bustling street markets and to do a waz up the wall.

Les Deux Fences, Number 27
The famous 'triangular fences' of Number 27 make for a spectacular sight, particularly on a still, moonlit night with nothing but the sound of crashing dustbin lids echoing around, like off the beginning of *Captain Scarlet*. Where the two fences join grows a large and imposing tree of some kind which, folk legend says, was used by Bugsy The Third to escape from Rex The Dog all that time ago. *C'est vrai.*

La Roof De La Shed De Number 56
Since its discovery by Big Town's petty bourgeoisie, La Roof De La Shed De Number 56 (or 'La Roof' as we called it before it became fashionable and ghastly) is now largely unbearable. Touristy and gimmicky, it's best avoided altogether.

The world, yesterday

WEEKEND BREAKS

You are all snuggly and warm. They are going totally frantic. Hahahaha…

● **IN A CARRIER BAG**
And you can rip it to shreds afterwards

● **IN THE LAUNDRY BASKET**
Be sure you don't end up wet and dizzy

● **IN A WARDROBE**
Shoes for poos!

● **UNDER THE BED**
Especially when your people are having sex. Jump on the bed when things start getting noisy

● **ON THE ROOF**
You can see them. They can't see you

● **NEXT DOOR**
New treats! Strokes galore! Piss where you want and run like bloody fuck!

● **IN A WALL CAVITY**
Mewl plaintively and loudly for extra fun

● **UP A TREE**
Be careful, though. What goes up may not be able to get down

● **IN A CAR WHEEL ARCH**
An entire weekend might be a little bit risky, actually

PARADISE

AT NUMBER 38?

You've heard the rumours. But is it really pussy paradise round the back of Number 38? We sent Tibbs to check it out. This is what he says he saw. Turn the page for his full report...

WHAT TIBBS SAW AT NUMBER 38

1) BUTTERFLIES

"Right, OK, the first thing I saw were the butterflies. But not ordinary butterflies. Oh no. These ones were about three times the size of normal ones, and when you chased them they sort of just gave up and fell into your mouth. And they didn't taste like chicken. They tasted like fish. Apart from the head, which tasted like chocolate. And they were about five or six times larger than normal butterflies, which are completely rubbish compared to these ones."

2) LOVELY RUG

"And then I was tired cos I'd eaten about 20 butterflies, which tasted like cheese, so I had a sleep on a lovely rug which was loads better than any rug I've ever slept on ever before ever."

3) BIRDS

"So then, right, there were these birds just hopping around and sort of singing, 'Eat me, eat me' and it was the best song I have ever heard. When I went up to them, they flapped about a bit, and then let me catch them and eat them. And they weren't the normal sort of birds you see, which are all brown and thin and don't have much meat on them and the best bit is when you crunch the skull and get all the brains. No, these birds were really fat and juicy and they tasted really great. Sort of like rabbit. With fish flakes. I ate three of them."

4) LOVELY CUSHION

"I got a bit sleepy after eating the tasty birds – I must have had about six or seven – so I went for a kip on this lovely cushion. It was a hundred times more comfy than the lovely rug. And it was made out of catnip. I had loads of great dreams, most of them about mice."

5) FOUNTAIN OF CREAM

"And while I was sleeping, I heard this big splashing noise, so I opened one eye and I saw this huge great fountain in the middle of the garden and out of it was coming all cream. Can you believe it? All cream coming out of a fountain!!! It was bloody lovely! And then I thought I saw a dog, so I bloody scarpered. It was really ace, though. Honest."

Chateau d'Oiseau

Where food gets very real

Unlike other so-called fast food establishments, our produce comes to you very fast and very fresh. In fact, you kill it yourself. All of our dishes are seasonal, with winter dishes being our speciality (the robins and bluetits are particularly sought after)

all our food may contain traces of nuts and seeds

FASHION

NECKING IT!

Nothing makes a more powerful statement about who you are than your collar. Whether it's a classic single tone or a splashy number in fun colours, make sure you choose the collar that's right for you...

Minski wears silver collar, £2.99

Minski wears pink collar, £2.99
Perry wears blue 'Stars' collar, £2.99

Perry wears green collar, £2.99

Minski wears dark pink collar, £2.99 (above)
and bright pink collar, £2.99 (right)

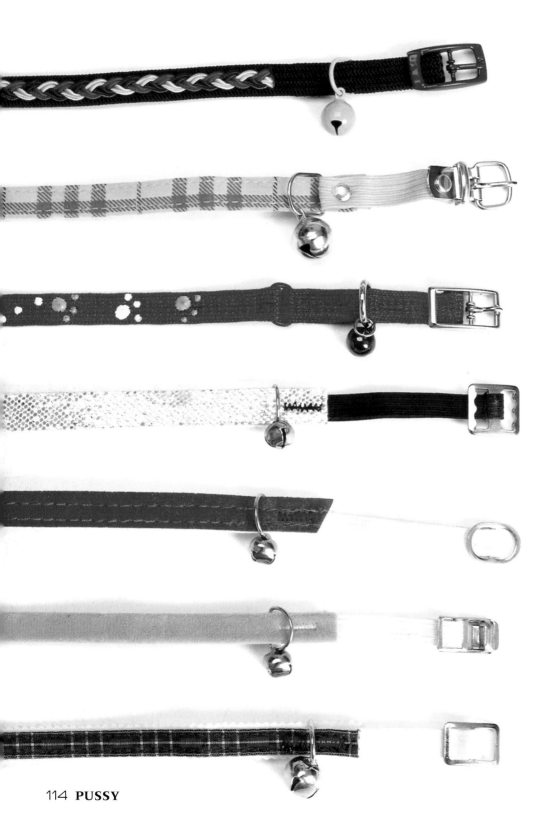

Minski wears yellow tartan collar, £2.99
Collars (left, top to bottom): black 'Lace' collar, £2.99; yellow tartan collar, £2.99; red 'Pawprints' collar, £2.99; silver collar, £2.99; dark pink collar, £2.99; green collar, £2.99; 'Scottie' tartan collar, £2.99

Stockists:
The Pet Shop, Main Street,
The Other Pet Shop, Little Road

GROOMIN[G]

A clean kitty is a happy kitty! This issue, we look at anal hygiene and flea combin[g]. We also have a poem about licking from Biggles The Poet

DON'T HAVE A HEINOUS ANUS
Three dos and a great big don't

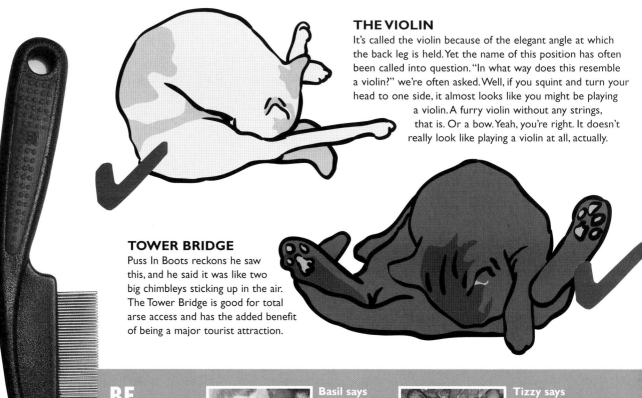

THE VIOLIN

It's called the violin because of the elegant angle at which the back leg is held. Yet the name of this position has often been called into question. "In what way does this resemble a violin?" we're often asked. Well, if you squint and turn your head to one side, it almost looks like you might be playing a violin. A furry violin without any strings, that is. Or a bow. Yeah, you're right. It doesn't really look like playing a violin at all, actually.

TOWER BRIDGE

Puss In Boots reckons he saw this, and he said it was like two big chimbleys sticking up in the air. The Tower Bridge is good for total arse access and has the added benefit of being a major tourist attraction.

BE BRUSHED OR GET STUFFED

Basil says
NO
"I won't let that thing anywhere near me and the last person who tried got a pawful of fives."

Tizzy says
YES
"Yep, I let my person give me a good old run through. Then I claw them for fun anyway."

MAKING A CHIMNEY

If you can imagine a chimney, only one not made with bricks, but out of fur, and shaped like a cat's leg, then you know why this particular position is called Making A Chimney (or Chimbley, if you prefer). Fine access to all that nasty claggy, but don't expect smoke to come billowing out of your paw. It ain't a real chimbley now, y'hear?

HELPING A FRIEND

This is out there, kitties. We don't want to see none of you pussies licking each other's arses. That would be bad. That there's dog behaviour – and we don't want none of that around here.

LICKY LICKY SANDPAPER STICKY

Being a poem about grooming. By Biggles (aged 5)

Licky, licky sandpaper sticky
Sticky licky, sandpaper licky
Sandpaper licky, sticky, licky
Sticky sandpaper licky, licky

Licky sandpaper, sticky, licky
Licky sandpaper, licky sticky
Sandpaper licky, sandpaper sticky
Licky licky, licky licky

[Biggles, seriously, is this going on much longer? – Ed]

Sandpaper, sandpaper, sticky, licky
Sandpaper, sandpaper, licky, sticky
Sandpaper, sandpaper, licky licky
Sandpaper, sandpaper, sticky sticky

[Give me one good reason why I shouldn't sack you – Ed]

GET READY 2 PARTY!

Four crucial grooming tips for a night on the tiles

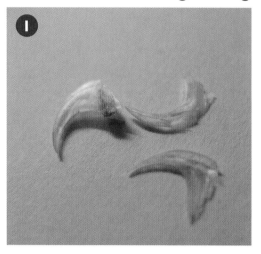

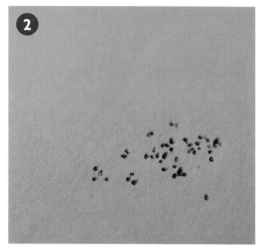

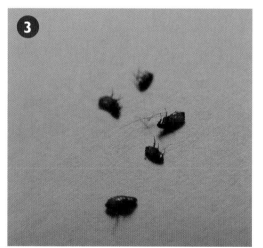

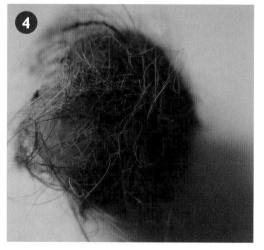

1. Get those loose claws off. It's not pleasant to see ugly lumps of claw (and bits of curtain and the back of the chair) when you are trying to impress her.

2. If things go well, you never know, you might get your ears licked. And although those girl cats like a bit of tom wax, ear mites taste very bitter and may ruin your chances.

3. Infesting your people's pad with millions of ghastly parasites that require public health officials to come in and bin all their soft furnishings? Good. Getting bitten during some serious lurve action? Bad.

4. If you happen to be 'a bit shaggy round the back', make sure you've got those fur balls up well before the rumpy-pumpy starts.

L'ORMIAOW

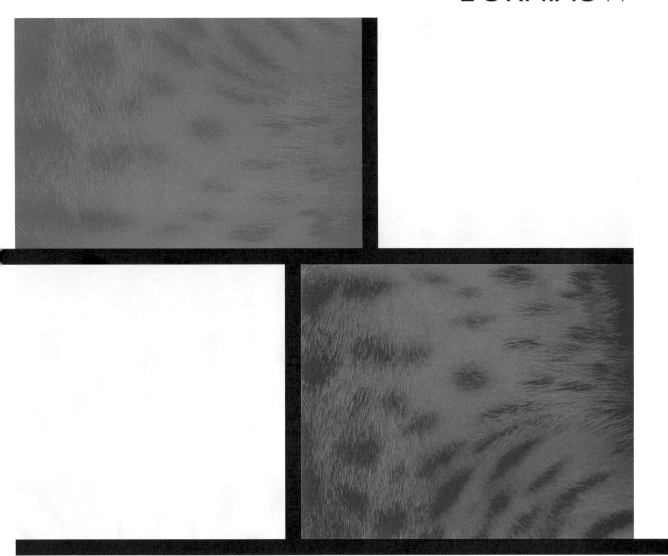

BECAUSE YOU'RE WORTHLESS

PROBLEMS

This issue, our Agony Aunt Prudence helps Suggsy, who just wants to be alone, and Ludo, who has got a really fucking long arm all of a sudden. If you have a problem you'd like Prudence to help you with, write to: Prudence, The Garden Shed, The House With The Red Door, Big Town M1 A0W

Dear Prudence

Prudence has received a letter from Suggsy The Kitten, who has been having some serious issues with Little Ben (one of his litter mates). Suggsy is at the end of his wits – as you can see in our fabulous photo reconstruction...

And so...

OOF!

ARGH!

I BEAT THE SHIT OUT OF IT AND IT STILL FARTS IN MY FACE

HELP ME, PRUDENCE, COS THIS IS DRIVING ME INSANE!! @&%*?!!

PRUDENCE WRITES:
Remember, Suggsy: 1) There is always a good chance that Little Ben is gonna get picked out in the Kitten Parade at the weekend. 2) You could get picked out in the Kitten Parade (just look extra cute and don't waz on the lovely people). 3) You can just stop whining, pull yourself together and grow up, you little twat.

Dear Prudence,
After three hours of solid dozing, I woke up to find my front leg had sort of melted down the back of the radiator. It's a total pisser. When I go out, I have a terrible limp, and all of the other cats laugh at me and call me Tripod. What should I do? Please help me, Prudence!
Ludo, Big Town

PRUDENCE WRITES:
Poor Ludo. Things have gone rather badly for you, haven't they? We all know how cruel our so-called 'friends' can be when we develop deformities or bits just fall off. Or, indeed, if parts of us suddenly melt and get very long. My thorough medical training and expert eye tells me that you are suffering from melty leg, technically known as *meltus legus*. What you need to do is pack some ice around the melty leg and make it go hard again. You will find that the cold will shrink the leg back to its original size. If that doesn't work, well, I'm all out of ideas, so you're on your own, Tripod Boy.

HOROSCOP

Spooky Sparkles, Pussy's one-eyed astrologer, consults the universe to see what the stars have in store for you...

Wooo! Wooo! Wooo! I am Spooky Sparkles, your conduit to the mystery of the stars! Wooo! Wooo! Come this way, and I will share the secrets of divining the future through the ancient and mysterious mystifying mysteries that have, erm, mystered everyone for ages. Wooo! Wooo!
[Get on with it, Dave – Ed].

Gemini (May. Or is it March? One of them, anyway)

As a Gemini, you are often pacing around your territory, dissatisfied, always thinking that something better is just round the corner. Well, IT'S NOT THERE! YOU ARE NOT GOING TO FIND A SECRET STASH OF SALMON! DEAL WITH IT! CATNIP DOES NOT GROW WILD IN THE GARDEN... It does? Does it really? Oh. Piss. Well, erm... Wooo! Wooo!

Saggitaurus (Which is, like, Christmas or something)

You are a lot like the Taurus cat (hence the name), but you're also a bit Saggi, too. And this means (in the mysterious mysteries of the horoscopical dimension) you fall over all the time. You need to be careful on or around the 14th, because you might fall into a dustbin and lose an eye.

Leo (Is it August? Leo? Anyway, Leo is a dog's name)

Shut up, Leo! Bloody dog. Will you stop barking? Wooo! Wooo! A lion? Leo is a lion? Now look, I agreed to write this thing out of the goodness of my heart, so stop taking the mickey. Lions, I ask you.

Taurus (Does this come after Aries? I think it does)

The Taurus pussy is the pussy who likes to stay home and curl up in front of the fire, lifting his head languidly from time to time, just to make sure that everyone is still there and see if it's time for dinner yet. But you must watch out over the next three weeks, because a big dog is going to break into your home and attack you. The dog will be wearing a flying helmet. I can see the name 'Snoopy'. Or maybe 'Snoop'. He will also be rapping. Oh, and you may lose an eye. Wooo! Wooo!

Cancer (June? October?)

Dingles is Cancer and he's the biggest bastard going. So, Dingles, watch out this month cos you're going to get a shit shower of really rubbish stuff happening to you, starting with your people buying tuna flavour Whiskas instead of rabbit. Ha! And that's not all. Me and Bilbo are going to duff you up next Tuesday. Wooo! Wooo!

Aquarius (This sounds like January. Don't ask me why, it just does. I said don't ask me why. Well, it's the water thing, isn't it? There's lots of water around in January, isn't there? It's because of the cheese. Oh, I don't know, do I?)

Erm. You'll start the month off well, with lots of sleeping and grooming and all that sort of stuff. Yay! But then things go badly wrong when you develop a nasty infection and you lose an eye. You might even lose both of them, which will make you blind. It will probably be for the best if you spend the whole month asleep, thereby not exposing your eyes to any infections, etc. Be careful of dustbins, too.

S

Aries *(March 21 – April 20)*

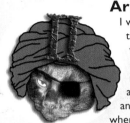

I will generally have a brilliant time this month and things will all go very well for me. On the 12th, I will have a particularly good morning hunting, and I will be able to place three mice, a bird and a rabbit on the back porch where they will be admired by my people, who will reward me with an hour of petting and some of those nice chocolate things that taste a bit like soil. Ace! And on the 17th, which is actually my birthday, you know, they will give me a huge pile of boss pressies cos I'm so super.

Pisces *(February, I expect)*

To you, it's all about fish, isn't it? Fishy this and fishy that. If you could be a fish, you would. You'd rather be swimming in a river with eyes on either side of your head than be a cat and chase mice and generally be a mammal. What's so great about fish, eh? OK, they taste good, but why actually be one? Listen, I will say this only once: water is nasty shite. You hear me? Water is nasty shite. WATER IS NASTY SHITE. You're bloody mad, you are. That's why you live on your own in that cardboard box down by the canal.

Scorpion *(Fairly certain this is when it gets cold. November?)*

There will be a nuclear war this month, and you and your fellow scorpions will be the only creatures still walking the face of the Earth. Wooo! Wooo! Hold on a minute... Actually, come to think about it, I might mean cockroaches. Is it cockroaches or scorpions that can survive nuclear war? Whatever. If it's cockroaches, then you'll probably be mainly eating fish and drinking milk this month. If it's scorpions then go back to that first bit I said.

Libra *(Don't know when this is. When haven't we had? OK, November and a bit of December, then)*

I can't stand this any more. Can I stop now? Oh, bloody hell. All right. There will be an earthquake this month and you will get hit by several bits of flying masonry. You might even lose an eye. *What?* It could happen! It *could*! You never know. I mean, the stars have prophesied these earthly events! Wooo! Wooo!

Capricorn One *(September-ish)*

This month you will think that you're going into space, only to be taken out of the big rocket seconds before the launch. You will then be ordered to fake the space mission by sinister people who make it clear that you will be put down if you refuse to co-operate. Unwilling to engage in this fraud, you escape, only to be hunted down like vermin. One of you, however, evades capture and turns up at their own funeral, thus blowing the lid on the whole cover-up. And that's where the film ends. Wooo! Wooo! Beware the black helicopters.

Virgo *(Might this be September, or have we already had September?)*

Wooo! Wooo! Beware the full moon this month, all you Virgos out there, for this is when the ghosts of all those innocent creatures come back to haunt the Virgo pussy cats that persecuted them in life. Wooo! Wooo! Hey, this is serious shit, dude. You really don't want to be having to deal with this. Trust me, I'm an astronaut. A million moth ghosts and a similar amount of mice ghosts will attack you, and make terrible things happen to your eye. Your left eye, probably. I suggest you do not leave the house for the whole of this month, so make sure that your person realises this and gets you a poo tray. Or perhaps not. Wooo! Wooo!

Send us piccies of your favourite chums. If you're lucky, we'll print one and make some insulting comment, and they can be the proud idiot on the garden fence who thinks they're famous.
Send your piccies to: Readers Mates, The Garden Shed, Blah Fucking Blah, Yadda Yadda BO LLX

Dotty (from Number 3)
She's a saucy little minx

Tabitha (from Number 69)
Apparently she still climbs

Lester's mate Brandy (The House With The Big Hedge)
What's going on here, Lester? Frankly, we're a little disturbed by this shot...

Bianca (sent in
Wow! Another a'
good mouse killer

Daphne Mae (from The Chippy)
She's cute - and you get free fish!

Didz (The House With That Shed)
Is it bathtime, baby? What???

Minnie
She's l
she's an

ATES

ONE FOR THE LADIES

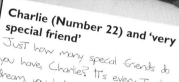

Charlie (Number 22) and 'very special friend'

Just how many special friends do you have, Charlie? It's every Tom's dream, you lucky bastard

at Number 18)

Bostin reckons she's a swlll

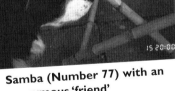

Samba (Number 77) with an anonymous 'friend'

Right, we only published This one as Samba's got a great Tree in his Territory and he says he will let us hang out in iT. BuT seriously, Samba, we've got To question your motivation on This one — iT's a frickin dog, maTe

Number 20)

chilled out here.. Bet s kinda gal

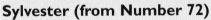

Sylvester (from Number 72)

OK, Sylvester, how many times do we have to open an envelope to find *yet another* picture of you showing your ridiculously visible bollocks? We know you're very proud of them and, in many ways, you're quite right to be very proud of them. They're a fine pair of corkers. A terrific set of nadgers. There's no doubt about that. But, y'know, there is a limit to the number of times we can print the same photo. Perhaps another three times, but that's it. No more, Sylvester, there's a good fellow.

ALSO FROM THE MAKERS OF PUSSY...

24 carrots

WARREN PEACE
feng shui for rabbits

Eco-friendly burrowing

What's <u>really</u> up, doc?

Discover your inner bunny

CARROTS   DIGGING   HOPPING   SHAGGING

ARF ARF
ARF ARF ARF A
ARF ARF ARF
ARF ARF ARF AR

ARF ARF ARF—

ARF ARF ARF AR
ARF ARF ARF ARF A

ARF A

THE
WHEEL

THE JOURNAL FOR RODENTS & SMALL FURRIES WORLDWIDE   issue no 1

DO YOU FEEL CAGED IN?

POUCHES, SAWDUST & SEEDS

IS LIFE JUST A TREADMILL?

IS TWO YEARS ENOUGH TO BUILD AN EMPIRE?

ARF ARF ARF ARF

Dear Newsagent,
Please reserve me a copy of:
WARREN PEACE / ARF / THE WHEEL
(delete as applicable, unless you want *Arf*,
in which case you're probably too stupid
to know what 'applicable' means)

Name: ....
Address: ....
            ....

FUR
cough
publishing

PUSSY CLASSIFIEDS

MOTHER MOUSE SEEN ENTERING SHED at No 38

Are you a sinner? Are you going to suffer in cat hell, where dogs will chase you for eternity?

Come to the **Pussy Tabernacle** and save your soul. Free milk.

◆ Ever felt there was something missing?
◆ Do you like orgies?
◆ Is yowling at the full moon your thing?
◆ Fancy being worshipped by people?

Join us for an informal discussion session: **The Ancient Egyptian Cult Of Basti,** Behind The Church Hall, Big Town

Chicks FOR FREE

WE BUY

Tuna, salmon, seafood, cheese. No questions asked. Good prices. Will collect. Contact **ED or ZIPPY**

IT'S HERE! Our AMAZING NEW product will CHANGE YOUR LIFE. And this one REALLY WORKS! It's not like the last one we sold, which was crap. Our CAT-FRIENDLY TIN OPENER is a MARVEL of modern TECHNOLOGICAL INNOVATION. IMAGINE! You'll be be able to open tins of CAT FOOD, TUNA, SALMON FLAKES and even SPAGHETTI HOOPS! Don't delay, apply for yours TODAY! HURRY! HURRY! HURRY! Box No. 436, Other Town

I NEED HELP!

Professional lady cat needs help. I am snowed under. Earn £££s! Or fishy treats if you prefer. Just come along any time and you'll find a welcome here.

The Gonk Manufacturing Co., Big Town

Have you ever considered a career in sitting around, doing nothing, being fed and petted? Look no further, your search is at an end! Pop in any time. Just don't tell anyone where you're going. There's no need for that.

The Gonk Manufacturing Co., Big Town

Unlock the secrets to accessing an unlimited supply of rotten old fish!

For a small fee, we will let you in on the special knowledge that has been the preserve of an elite few for generations. Never go hungry again! Rotten old fish and sometimes prawns, too!

Come round the back of the fishmongers after 11.

PSYCHO?

Get non-prescription mood controlling medication from me. Discreet service.

Ask for Sidney at The Big Shed

COMBAT KITTY

PUT THE WIZE

IN STREETWIZE

MAXIMUM FLUFFING UP
BACKING DOWN AND SAVING FACE
THE TEN-MINUTE STARE
PLUS
ADVANCED FLUFFING UP, SICKING UP & POST-COMBAT SLEEPING
NO FARMIES PLEASE - BRING A TIN

* We also run advanced courses in "Superior Sleeping" and "Advanced Sicking Up"

CAT 22

IMPROVE YOUR HUNTING CREDENTIALS

Courses in:
The Easy Catch
Prolonging the Kill
Entrail Placement
Sicking Up

* We also run advanced courses in "Superior Sleeping" and "Advanced Sicking Up"

SUMMER FUN
"Summer Heat"
People away
and a split
pond liner

The House With The Apple Tree

MASSIVE
OPPORTUNITY

OPEN AIR VENT AT THE BABY CHICKEN FARM

TOMCAT at No. 63
seeks clean-living lady
cat for a no commitment
mating anytime soon

Pussy was conceived and created by Steven Appleton, Christopher Dawes, Mark Roland and Paul Thompson
Studio photography by Dave Guttridge at The Photographic Unit, Norwich

Support and assistance: Emily Groom, Kaoru Sakurai, Susie Mair, Jan Newell and Antony Topping

Cat people: Deborah Adams, Fiona Andreanelli, Amy Barratt, Lucy Beaumont, John Birrell, Miriam Brightman, Ted Cox, Greg Curtis, Todd & Donna Faller, Julie Garrod, Janice & Allan Hamer, Sandra Hawe, Judi Hayes, Cerian Hutchings, Michèle Hutchison, Kate Jennings, Andrew Jervis, Steph Kedik, Jon Kitson, Notty Nottingham, Lesley Ormrod, John Sparrowhawk, Terry Pink, Grace Richardson, Heloise Saunders, Lindsay Scandrett, Angela Seed, Judith Welsh and Reuben Youngblood.

TRANSWORLD PUBLISHERS
61-63 Uxbridge Road, London W5 5SA, a division of The Random House Group Ltd

RANDOM HOUSE AUSTRALIA (PTY) LTD
20 Alfred Street, Milsons Point, Sydney, New South Wales 2061, Australia

RANDOM HOUSE NEW ZEALAND LTD
18 Poland Road, Glenfield, Auckland 10, New Zealand

RANDOM HOUSE SOUTH AFRICA (PTY) LTD
Endulini, 5a Jubilee Road, Parktown 2193, South Africa

Published 2004 by Bantam Press, a division of Transworld Publishers

Copyright © Steven Appleton, Christopher Dawes, Mark Roland and Paul Thompson 2004

The right of Steven Appleton, Christopher Dawes, Mark Roland and Paul Thompson to be identified as the authors of this work has been asserted in accordance with sections 77 and 78 of the Copyright, Designs and Patents Act 1988.

A catalogue record for this book is available from the British Library.
ISBN 0593 05346X

Printed in Germany

1 3 5 7 9 10 8 6 4 2

Papers used by Transworld Publishers are natural, recyclable products made from wood grown in sustainable forests.
The manufacturing processes conform to the environmental regulations of the country of origin.